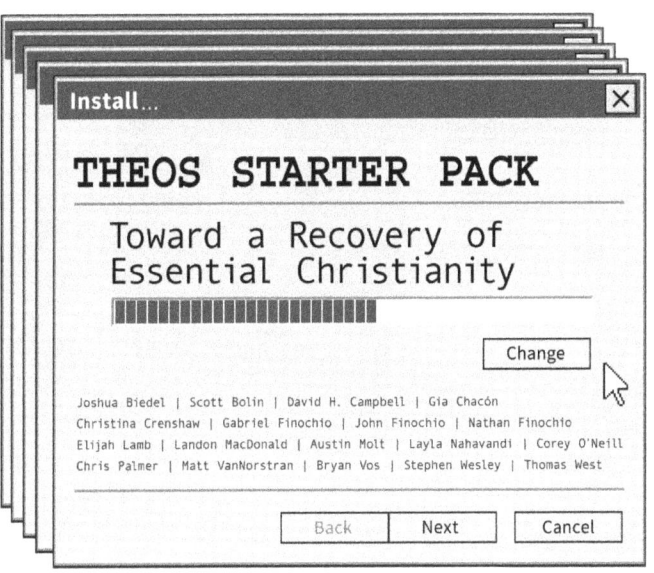

Install...

THEOS STARTER PACK

Toward a Recovery of Essential Christianity

Change

Joshua Biedel | Scott Bolin | David H. Campbell | Gia Chacón
Christina Crenshaw | Gabriel Finochio | John Finochio | Nathan Finochio
Elijah Lamb | Landon MacDonald | Austin Molt | Layla Nahavandi | Corey O'Neill
Chris Palmer | Matt VanNorstran | Bryan Vos | Stephen Wesley | Thomas West

Back Next Cancel

Edited by:
NATHAN FINOCHIO
AND
CHRIS PALMER

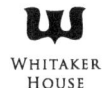

WHITAKER HOUSE

Unless otherwise indicated, all Scripture quotations are taken from *The Holy Bible, English Standard Version*, © 2016, 2001, 2000, 1995 by Crossway Bibles, a division of Good News Publishers. Used by permission. All rights reserved. Scripture quotations marked (MEV) are taken from *The Holy Bible, Modern English Version*. Copyright © 2014 by Military Bible Association. Published and distributed by Charisma House. All rights reserved. Scripture quotations marked (NIV) are taken from the *Holy Bible, New International Version*®, NIV®, © 1973, 1978, 1984, 2011 by Biblica, Inc.® Used by permission of Zondervan. All rights reserved worldwide. www.zondervan.com. The "NIV" and "New International Version" are trademarks registered in the United States Patent and Trademark Office by Biblica, Inc.® Scripture quotations marked (KJV) are taken from the King James Version of the Holy Bible.

Boldface type in the Scripture quotations indicates the authors' emphasis.

THEOS STARTER PACK
Toward a Recovery of Essential Christianity

Edited by Nathan Finochio and Chris Palmer

www.theosu.ca
www.instagram.com/theosuniversity
www.facebook.com/theosuniversity

ISBN: 979-8-88769-004-9
eBook ISBN: 979-8-88769-005-6
Printed in the United States of America
© 2023 TheosU

Whitaker House
1030 Hunt Valley Circle
New Kensington, PA 15068
www.whitakerhouse.com

Library of Congress Control Number: 2023931882

No part of this book may be reproduced or transmitted in any form or by any means, electronic or mechanical—including photocopying, recording, or by any information storage and retrieval system—without permission in writing from the publisher. Please direct your inquiries to permissionseditor@whitakerhouse.com.

1 2 3 4 5 6 7 8 9 10 11 ⨆ 30 29 28 27 26 25 24 23

CONTENTS

Introduction 7
  1. Recovering the Big Story | *Nathan Finochio* 11
  2. Recovering the Way We Teach | *Scott Bolin and Bryan Vos* 17
  3. Recovering Dogma | *Gabriel Finochio* 27
  4. Recovering the Gospel | *Thomas West* 37
  5. Recovering Reconciliation | *Stephen Wesley* 47
  6. Recovering Apocalyptic | *Chris Palmer* 57
  7. Recovering Revelation | *David H. Campbell* 67
  8. Recovering Worship | *Layla Nahavandi* 77
  9. Recovering the Spirit | *John Finochio* 87
10. Recovering Our Language | *Elijah Lamb* 97
11. Recovering History | *Joshua Biedel* 107
12. Recovering Our Youth | *Austin Molt* 117
13. Recovering the Minor Prophets | *Landon MacDonald* 125
14. Recovering Creation | *Matt VanNorstran* 135
15. Recovering Justice: Doing Good for God's Glory |
    Christina Crenshaw 147
16. Recovering Our Care for the Persecuted | *Gia Chacón* 157
17. Recovering Our Battle Against Sin | *David H. Campbell* 167
18. Recovering the Way We Learn | *Corey O'Neill* 177

19. Recovering Christ as King | *Nathan Finochio* 187
20. Recovering Mystery | *Chris Palmer* 197

Last Words 209
About the Authors 211

INTRODUCTION

If you're on social media, you can't escape memes—those images or videos with captions designed to amuse or inform.

Starter packs take memes a few steps further. In its most primitive form, a starter pack is a collage of four images, although sophisticated starter packs can have more. The images serve as essential items that accurately describe the subject of the pack. If properly executed, the carefully chosen images not only point out what's obvious, but also what's ironic and uncomfortable.

At TheosU, we operate a meme page (@theosU_memes) where we've specialized in starter packs since AD 2020. All our starter packs are handcrafted using original material and natural components to ensure that our subscribers are getting the most accurate description possible. Our subscribers' favorites include:

- *The Assistant Pastor starter pack*: a 2004 Ford Taurus; a sale in the Kohl's men's department; a notice of overdraft fees from the bank; a pack of Marlboro cigarettes
- *End Time Prophecy Teacher starter pack*: a forty-foot wall chart on the eras of dispensation; a MAGA hat; a shofar; a dress shirt with armpit stains
- *Former Charismatic starter pack*: a John MacArthur study Bible; a flannel shirt; a podcast mic; a *Soli Deo Gloria* tattoo

Like art, they are open for interpretation:

- Assistant pastors are overworked and underpaid.

- End time prophecy teachers are so fixated on what happens to America and Israel that they lose their self-awareness.
- Former charismatics turn spiteful toward the movement, demonstrating, once again, the same extremism that got them in the hyper-charismatic ditch in the first place.

The starter pack prompts you to think, "So this is what it's come to, has it?"

Welcome to *Theos Starter Pack*.

Only, this isn't a meme. It's a book.

Instead of an assortment of images, we've got an assortment of twenty essays.

In them, our authors discuss a variety of topics we feel are of utmost importance, well-deserving of attention, and essential to Christianity.

The aim of *this* starter pack is to prompt our readers to think about *why* they might think about these topics the way they do. Why are things the way they are? And how has it come this?

Some essays provoke. Some pry. They might make you chuckle with hilarity or cringe with discomfort. Maybe you'll be consoled or encouraged. Or maybe you'll take to the Amazon reviews and let your inner Karen rage.

A little backstory.

In 2021, TheosU organized an online conference and invited scholars, pastors, and professors to address theological topics with the local church in mind. For three days, the presenters shared their knowledge and experience. They addressed issues such as deconstruction, the adverse effects of post-modernity, poor hermeneutics, and trends among evangelicals that veer away from the wisdom of the historical church. These things have led to the devaluation and compromise of convention and orthodoxy within twenty-first century, Western evangelical circles.

The response was striking. But questions emerged. Namely, what does tradition say? How exactly has it been lost in local church teaching and practices? Can it be recovered, at least within our milieu?

Theos Starter Pack begins to answer those questions, not from self-interest, but from a point of view influenced by the historical church throughout the millennia. By looking back to examples from early Christianity, each author takes up an issue, airs their grievance, and proposes a solution of sorts that contributes *first thoughts* toward recovering the essential aspect of Christianity they are discussing from out of the clutches of error, ignorance, and indifference.

All that to say, it's a start. A starter pack. The beginning of a discussion about God and theology by an interesting motley crew of Bible geeks and church practitioners—your friends here at TheosU.

The authors have chosen areas where they have already demonstrated competence either through ministry tenure, academic contribution, or professional experience. Some are scholars. Others are pastors. Some are missionaries. Some are teachers. They include social media influencers and Christian advocates. Some authors are funny. Others are earnest. You'll hear sarcasm and savagery, solemness and sincerity, seriousness and silliness.

And yet they all have something in common: none of them are armchair thinkers, calling the plays from their living room couch. Everyone is active in ministry, serving the local church, which they love fervently, despite her imperfections. That love drives each author. Hopefully, it's felt on every page and within each word.

You can read this book however you'd like. March straight through it, like a standard piece of nonfiction, or hop around to essays that grab your interest. The only thing we do recommend is that you read each essay—*if* you want the total picture this starter pack offers.

Is *Theos Starter Pack* like Thomas Aquinas's *Summa Theologica*? John Calvin's *Institutes of the Christian Religion*? Or perhaps Karl Barth's *Church Dogmatics*?

Nah. But you'll probably snicker more reading this book.

And who knows? Maybe after reading this, you might be inspired to begin reading works of real theological greatness. That's our hope, at least.

Good studying,

Nathan Finochio and Chris Palmer
TheosU

1

RECOVERING THE BIG STORY

NATHAN FINOCHIO

I was around fourteen years old the first time I heard Pastor Jude Fouquier preach. It was like hearing "Thriller" for the first time. I was in Utica, New York, at Generation Youth Conference hosted by Mike Servello Jr., in a room full of teens from all over the Northeastern United States and Canada. The room was heavy with sweat and carbon dioxide; we had just screamed praise songs at the top of our lungs for forty-five minutes. Now it was preaching time. Pastor Jude, then a forty-year-old Louisiana lightning rod, was loud, hilarious, and passionate. And he talked to us about reading the Bible.

He began his sermon by giving a comedic account of a recent accident he'd had at the gym in which he had managed to drop a fifty-pound weight on his big toe, fragmenting the bone like a well-marked clay pigeon. Upon having surgery to put the bone back together, he was forbidden by doctors to put any weight on it for three months. And being a man who has ants in his pants, he channeled all of his energy into reading the entire Bible in thirty days for three months.

I remember being impressed with the feat and making a mental note as a teenager that I would at some point in my adult years do that very thing, sans complete destruction of the hallux. And I kept that promise when I turned thirty-one—which felt like the right year to do something extreme and manly and daring. And to my surprise, I accomplished the task.

At the time, I lived in the East Village of Manhattan—in a 225-square-foot shack—with my young wife, Jasmine. And I routinely walked across the island every day to a studio owned by my friends in the West Village. I would prayer-walk down 12th Street every day that January and complete my Bible reading in the solitude of the studio. It took about one or two hours, depending on the day, and I quickly became addicted to the sense of momentum at finishing forty chapters a day. That momentum quickly snowballed into half the Bible in fifteen days—an uproarious thought for your average Christian.

It was invigorating.

I'd never been a very consistent Bible reader before, probably because I'm not a nine-to-five kind of guy; I'm more project based. It's how I'm wired—for sprints, not long distances. But I had read the Bible lots and knew the Bible very well as a Bible college grad. Yet I had never read it right through.

What I began to notice during this thirty-day experiment was my attention to things I had never seen collectively. All of my Bible reading and study had been a parsing—it was an examination of the leaves of the tree and not the tree itself. To put it colloquially, I was missing the forest for the tree.

The Bible is a book. And yes, it is also a collection of books. But it's a book—it's one big story.

And I was missing the big picture—not surprisingly, as big things have a way of hiding better than small things. Like the shape of the earth.

As I began to read the Bible quickly in that short amount of time, I began to see the topography of Scripture—the giant movements in salvation history—and couldn't help but note the recognition and repetition of themes that form a thread throughout holy writ. The theologians call this canonical thinking, and it's really helpful as someone trying to interpret Scripture.

Why? Because every verse in the Bible has an immediate context—which helps us determine what that author was trying to say in that specific instance—but also a much larger context, the context of the *"whole counsel of God,"* to borrow from Paul in Acts 20:27.

The Bible patterns itself this way also. David quotes Moses; the prophets quote Moses; Jesus quotes David, the prophets, and Moses; and Paul and the rest of the New Testament writers do the same. This is what scholars call intertextuality; these authors are not only thinking canonically but they are pulling specifically from other inspired sources verbatim and building upon previous Spirit revelation. This is particularly important for New Testament authors like Matthew, who continually employs the phrase "to fulfill what was spoken" as a proof that Jesus Christ is the fulfillment of the Law and Prophets. (See, for example, Matthew 1:22; 2:15, 17, 23.) Jesus Himself famously fights Satan with, *"It is written"* (Matthew 4:3–10) and quotes the Old Testament as an authoritative rebuke to Satan's eisegetical prompts.

The Bible is so large and its genres so varied that the impatient modern reader can easily pass it off as a disjointed, unconnected scrapbook of ancient self-help axioms. And this type of lazy dismissal is at the expense of the reader, who fails to see it as a mosaic or puzzle that forms a large yet overt and clear portrait of a King who loves His people and won't suffer their unraveling any further.

And reading the Bible in thirty days helps me see the big picture.

Before I started doing *the shred*, which is how I've cheekily branded the annual January ordeal online, I too was caught up in a great deal of theological minutiae. I always felt overwhelmed by complexity because in my estimation, there were a thousand hills that I needed to understand and then die upon. I suppose that's the ideological gymnastic called Bible college in a nutshell. But the Bible is much simpler than that. And seeing the whole tree of redemption helps inform the many doctrines, answering the genesis of them, and giving us the invaluable *why*.

A CRISIS

The Bible is like Shakespeare—oft quoted, seldom read. I cringe when I hear Jordan Peterson—perhaps one of the greatest Western intellectuals alive—attempt to quote Scripture. I suppose paraphrasing means the content has actually sunk in, but when the paraphrase is nowhere near the meaning, we have a problem.

The Bible isn't read today—not by our greatest intellectuals and not by our churches. And when it is read, it's apportioned devotionally, as if it's a magic cookie that delivers all of its power in tiny bites. Reading the Bible in any portion is good and little is better than none. But I don't know if demanding that it be magic immediately in isolated, disjointed readings is where its true power lies.

"What does this mean to me?" is not the first question we should be asking of an isolated chapter every day.

At least Peterson thinks on a grand scale in his archetypal approach to the Bible, saying, "This is an ancient book, and if I read as a psychologist I will be able to pull universals from this book." Some of these observations are fascinating and can be insightful regarding the relational dynamics and possible motivations of such-and-such a character in the narratives. But once again, if we miss the larger picture of Scripture that the authors are trying to paint, we've missed everything. There's no power in understanding Jacob's father wounds; there's power in the personal God of Jacob. The Bible can certainly give you wisdom for living, but to view it only in those terms is reductionistic at worst and self-help at best.

Swinging from the dialectical of Peterson, we grasp the vine of Friedrich Schleiermacher's "Abhängigkeit," or in lay terms, *the feels*. Peterson doesn't care about the feels; he cares about the facts of reality—and believes Scripture illustrates cold hard truth in its many triumphs and tragedies. If you don't confront the chaos, slay the dragon, and take your pills, you'll end up like Samson.

But the German higher critics like Schleiermacher and Rudolf Bultmann really love the feels, and they believe that you can sense God in the preaching of the Bible even though the Bible is not historically true and is probably just myth. They put a big emphasis on the feelings we get from Scripture.

Enter Jacques Derrida, who believes that meaning is local to the reader. Combine Schleiermacher with Derrida, and you have what constitutes the average evangelical Bible reader: "The Bible gives me the feels—particularly when I read it as a self-absorbed autocrat who wields all interpretive power injunctively. What this means to me in this exact moment of time, in the midst of my personal and interpersonal goings on, is deeply profound. I don't care what it means—I care what it means to me."

And of course, the Holy Spirit gets the credit for this hot mess.

This isn't happening here and there; this is the dominant practice of biblical consumption, and not just because progressive Christians advocate for this, but because orthodox evangelicals practice this in their pulpits by never letting the meaning of a passage get in the way of a good reboot. The congregation is conditioned by this approach and takes creative liberties devotionally where the preacher exhibits creative liberties homiletically.

Now you might ask, "What exactly are you advocating for here, Nathan? That everyone become a biblical scholar?"

Would that all of God's people prophesy! But no, that's not what I'm saying either. Because lots of Scripture is accessible through prima facie readings. That being said, it's also an ancient book, a large story, and we'll need to be patient in our reading.

So, yes, we need to learn the grammatical, historical, canonical method. We should do our best to become aware of the author's intent, the intended audience, and the context of every passage. But let's not forget that the context of every book of the Bible is the Bible itself. And this is where I believe we have lost our way.

Reading the Bible as a whole book immediately decentralizes the individual reader quite organically, in the same way reading any great work of fiction deposes the self-consumed despot and immerses the reader in the world of the characters. We are transported to Canaan by Moses in the same way that we are translated to Narnia by C. S. Lewis—if we will read long enough.

2

RECOVERING THE WAY WE TEACH

SCOTT BOLIN AND BRYAN VOS

A wise man once said, "When you are tired of saying it, they are just starting to hear it." That remark has proved to be invaluable to us throughout our time in ministry and higher education. It holds within it a truth that we all know too well: learning is a process, and it's rarely instantaneous.

This truth has led many pastors to utilize various pneumonic devices and wordplay to drive home their messages. It has led teachers and professors to use songs and visual examples to reiterate their points. It has led various technology companies to develop gamified learning platforms in an effort to access pleasure parts of the brain to make education more engaging.

Throughout history, we have always wrestled with the best way to teach.

It can often seem like these attempts to enhance the learning experience have been used and reused to the point that they're no longer useful. As a church volunteer or staff member, you become accustomed to hearing every pastor or leader's latest list of twelve whys, ten hows, or eight whats of leadership. It seems we have mistaken simplicity for sophistication.

The same can be said for higher education. In most lecture halls across the country, professors are still using the same auditory approach to teaching that they experienced fifty-some years ago. However, now we know much more about learning than we did when the modern universities were built. Today, we recognize that there are many ways in which people learn.

Where once we had modern knowledge of education to work with, we now have modern entertainment to compete against. There's a world of entertainment at our fingertips available through various streaming platforms. Netflix has consistently claimed the top spot among streaming providers, boasting approximately 220 million subscribers as of 2020.[1] In comparison, total enrollment at U.S. colleges and universities is approximately 19.4 million students as of 2020.[2]

But it's not just streaming platforms that make up the entertainment industry. There is a drastic increase in gaming that cannot be ignored. It is estimated that there will be over three billion gamers worldwide by 2023.[3] Investors and brands are flocking to the new opportunities within gaming and esports to turn a profit in this rapidly evolving industry. Games like *Fortnite* have gained worldwide popularity as various professional athletes and celebrities have made a side career through online streaming and competition. *Fortnite* changed the way that battle royale games were seen, incorporating a free/premium game model that has generated over $20 billion in in-game purchases since its launch. *Fortnite* has won awards globally and continues to see millions of active users daily.

It was through *Fortnite* that the story of Theos Seminary really began. In a conversation with Nathan Finochio, we shared our frustration that theology couldn't be delivered in a format that is as engaging as our shared games of *Fortnite*. After all, we and millions of others are enticed by *Fortnite*

---

1. Sandra Pattison, "35 Streaming Services Statistics You Need to Know in 2022," Cloudwards, last modified May 29, 2022; www.cloudwards.net/streaming-services-statistics.
2. "Back-to-School Statistics," National Center for Education Statistics; nces.ed.gov/fastfacts/display.asp?id=372.
3. Tom Wijman, "Three Billion Players by 2023: Engagement and Revenues Continue to Thrive Across the Global Games Market," *Newzoo*, June 25, 2020; newzoo.com/insights/articles/games-market-engagement-revenues-trends-2020-2023-gaming-report.

through its gamified elements of teamwork, competition, progression tracking, unlockable rewards, and so much more. Players can accomplish something and gain the rewards and unlockables to show their success. This was a new idea in comparison with successful games of old. In *Fortnite* and in many new games since then, a player's experience and skill can be easily identified by what the player is wearing within the game.

This idea sounds oddly familiar to higher education. Through dedicated study and preparation, proving yourself through tests and trials, you can emerge victorious on a stage in front of thousands who watch you receive the coveted degree. *Victory royale.* For us, these two experiences were inseparable. Why is it that education gets more expensive each year, yet there is no expectation from the consumer that the experience will get any better or innovative? In the gaming world, there is public outrage if the latest *Halo* game doesn't have a battle royale mode.

At TheosU and Theos Seminary, we aim to incorporate the strengths of gamification and rich user experience into the study of theology. We want to combine great theologians and resources, curating them in a way that motivates the average Christian to study their Bible again. We want subscribers to be able to stop and rewind through engaging video content while utilizing a robust Logos package to guide their study through TheosU. We want students to collaborate with their peers across the world regarding their paper on the Pauline Epistles, aiming for their best academic work in order to unlock their latest achievement and thus progress forward in their degree map—which looks a lot like Middle Earth—at Theos Seminary.

The path to gamified and engaging theological innovation is set, but there are things that we must first address. Above the fun and games (literally), we have a commitment on our team to remain biblically sound. We place the highest priority on the local church and want to ensure that our path forward is about her rather than the almighty dollar. We can see throughout history that many great Christian movements started great innovative universities, starting with Harvard in 1636. Harvard was the first university in the United States of America. Christians were instrumental in pioneering major societal support systems such as hospitals and libraries; with Harvard, they pioneered something that would become the foundation of higher education.[4]

Our goal from the beginning was to create an affordable and accessible alternative to the expensive private universities across America that offer poor scholarship and subpar master of divinity degrees. These schools have largely fallen victim to the peripheral ideologies that have crept into lecture halls and research papers, resulting in Bible degrees that lack formative substance. Many of these programs don't teach biblical languages, and their course curriculums have no grounding in the historical church. Our hope is that the commonly heard voice of the faculty and platforms of TheosU and Theos Seminary is not an echo chamber of ideas, but a shared conviction that the Bible is authoritative and the local church is God's plan for the world.

We see an opportunity to provide crucial support systems to believers around the world. What began as a streaming alternative organically became an ecosystem of like-minded believers, which we now affectionately call Theos Universe. For a lack of better terminology, this describes our continuously growing world that is made up of local church pastors and leaders seeking others to walk beside. TheosU and Theos Seminary includes a network of like-minded churches, a meme page, podcasts, an online conference, an in-person leader retreat, and more. We believe that the way we learn has to extend beyond our study time and into our conversations. *Our beliefs and convictions can be shared through a meme as well as through an academic paper.*

If we had a favorite Gospel, it would have to be the Gospel of Luke because of his careful preparation and explanation of the good news. His opening verses provide an insightful approach that is still relevant to us today as modern believers:

> *Inasmuch as many have undertaken to compile a narrative of the things that have been accomplished among us, just as those who from the beginning were eyewitnesses and ministers of the word delivered them to us, it seemed good to me also, having followed all things closely for some time past, to write an orderly account for you, most*

---

4. "The History of Harvard," Harvard University, www.harvard.edu/about/history.

excellent Theophilus, that you may have certainty concerning the things you have been taught. (Luke 1:1–4)

In these verses, Luke explains that he has done his due diligence to ensure that what he is about to provide is accurate. Throughout Luke's Gospel, we can see how hard he worked at this, from his interview accounts with Mary, the mother of Jesus, to the firsthand information that Luke would have had to seek out for himself, going straight to the source. There is a level of professionalism in Luke's Gospel that provides credibility to his writing. He places a high value on accuracy.

That burden is still ours today as Christians. We should take very seriously the communication of the Gospels and the training of Christian pastors and leaders.

For the kingdom of God to advance, we should heed the Scriptures regarding the stewardship of the bride of Christ and God's people. As Luke invested time and preparation into his Gospel, we should invest time and preparation into our lives as a gospel unto the world. Our theological education is more important than any other field of study because it dictates our ability to influence eternity for others. We would be selfish not to show ourselves as well-studied believers, being prepared to give an account as Peter suggests:

In your hearts honor Christ the Lord as holy, always being prepared to make a defense to anyone who asks you for a reason for the hope that is in you; yet do it with gentleness and respect. (1 Peter 3:15)

John Wesley was an excellent example of this stewardship, yet also an example of innovation. Wesley could be described as a traditionalist in his heart for the church, yet an innovator in his frustration with religion for religious sake. He maintained credibility as an Anglican minister while asking healthy questions about the structure and operation of the church. His unwavering commitment to essentials and openness to innovation of nonessentials led to the birth and ongoing growth of Wesleyanism.

Wesley provided a quadrilateral approach for the interpretation of faith. He first prioritized Scripture as a source. After Scripture has been reviewed, his next priority was tradition. Once tradition has been exhausted, one can then move on to their own reasoning and their personal experience. We value this approach because so much of what we hold to be crucial to our Christian faith was verified and upheld by the church fathers, who preserved the biblical text and ensured the truth was passed on. Because of their important role in Christianity, it is imperative that believers become acquainted with their lives.

Origen Adamantius wrote of the value of education in *Contra Celsum*, an apologetic Greek writing. He suggests that education is the pathway to virtue and knowledge, calling it the one stable and permanent reality.[5] His suggestion further iterates the point that our education as Christians goes beyond an attainment of temporary knowledge; it is an eternal endeavor through which the kingdom of God may be expanded.

There has been an alarming trend of decreasing enrollments across seminaries for years now.[6] While we can blame the secularization of society, we must surely take a hard look at the model of modern theological education. The widely accepted barriers to education in general are time and money. So how do we take the weighty responsibility and orchestrate a generational shift back toward education?

For many, higher education has an enormous time constraint that cannot be avoided. In order for someone to get a degree, they must pay with their time. For a traditional undergraduate student, this requires their full-time dedication for two to four years. For an adult learner, however, this time must be accumulated outside their full-time job, often resulting in online or night courses. Various institutions have taken innovative approaches to solve the issue of time. The University of Phoenix, for example, has pioneered short courses, foregoing the traditional sixteen-week approach. EdX has made micro credentials an acceptable option for someone wanting subject mastery without a four-year timeline or a mountain of debt.

But what about money?

---

5. Origen Adamantius, *Contra Celsum*, III, 49, 12.
6. Frederick Schmidt, "Navigating the Decline of America's Seminaries," *Progressive Christian*, May 17, 2022; www.patheos.com/blogs/whatgodwantsforyourlife/2022/05/navigating-the-decline-of-americas-seminaries.

For the 2021–2022 school year, tuition at the average private university in America was $35,852 per year.[7] The average cost of room and board on a private university campus in America was $10,089.[8] At $45,941 per year for tuition, room, and board, before associated books and fees, the average private university bachelor's degree cost $183,764. And just 25 percent of the courses students take to earn that degree are related to their major. The hopeful student who just enrolled at his local Christian university for his Bachelor of Arts in Youth Ministries is in for a rude awakening when he graduates.

But what about scholarships?

Ah, yes, the beloved free money that rides in on a white stallion to pay my bills and allow me to get a Christian education. The truth is, only 7 percent of students will receive a scholarship, and the average scholarship amounts to $7,400.[9] There are other sources of financial aid, such as the Pell Grant, which gives students up to $6,495 a year—assuming they meet all of the requirements and their parents' income is low enough.[10] By the time they graduate, the average degree holder from a private university—including the hopeful student who can now join the ranks of youth ministers—now has an average debt of $54,921.[11] When interest payments on college loans are added in, you can see where the trouble begins.

With a system like this, how can we expect the next generation of pastors and leaders to step up and view ministry as a career possibility, filling pulpits for another generation?

Higher education observer and author Jeffrey J. Selingo has been sounding the alarm on this issue for some time now. In his book *College (Un)bound*, he unpacks the case for higher education innovation and highlights many who are leading the way. Selingo points out that many colleges

---

7. Melanie Hanson, "Scholarship Statistics," EducationData.org, November 5, 2022; educationdata.org/scholarship-statistics.
8. Max Fay, "Dorm vs. Apartment: Which Is Cheaper," Debt.org, December 16, 2021; www.debt.org/students/dorm-vs-apartment.
9. Melanie Hanson, "Scholarship Statistics," EducationData.org, November 5, 2022; educationdata.org/scholarship-statistics.
10. "Pell Grant Eligibility: How to Determine If You Qualify," College Foundation Inc., accessed December 2, 2022; ncassist.cfnc.org/ncassistInfo/pell-grant-eligibility.
11. Melanie Hanson, "Average Student Loan Debt," EducationData.org, January 22, 2023; educationdata.org/average-student-loan-debt.

and universities pitch their degree programs as if they were mere products and seek students as their consumers. He notes:

> Colleges have adopted the selling techniques used in marketing toothpaste, movies, and cars. Universities have doled out big dollars in recent years to develop branding campaigns, pitching their wares to potential students.[12]

This perspective is sobering and is the very reason for our work at TheosU and Theos Seminary.

THE THEOSU SOLUTION

So, what are we doing about this? There is a clear need for theological and biblical higher education. There is a clear problem with the financial model of these degrees (and many others) and how that impacts a graduate who feels called to full-time ministry. Additionally, society values entertainment over education, with a vast number of people indulging in movies and comedy series rather than engaging with their faith.

At TheosU, we have incorporated content delivery through a streaming platform with short and intentional sections of lectures. We have taken the meat and potatoes and cut it up into bite-sized amounts. We continue to upload content that is culturally relevant as well as virtue producing. As we noticed that our content was beginning to gain traction, we shifted our focus to the institution of education. We needed a way to provide credible degrees to the average person, whether they feel called to ministry or not.

Theos Seminary incorporates our content from TheosU, immersing students in a learning management system where they can interact with peers from around the world. Together, students can collaborate on assignments on our community boards or within weekly live sessions called Theos Nights. Students take part in rigorous assignments, many of which would be considered graduate level at some of the private universities around the world. Our housing system is gamified, allowing students to be sorted into one of four student houses where they can engage in competitions and build a network of fellow pastors and leaders. Whether pursuing a

---

12. Jeffrey J. Selingo, *College (Un)bound: The Future of Higher Education and What It Means for Students* (New York: Houghton Mifflin Harcourt, 2013).

certificate, undergraduate degree, or graduate degree, students in Theos Seminary are becoming well rounded scholars in their own right.

The cost is as inexpensive as we can make it. We have incorporated a similar subscription pricing model to that found within TheosU. Seminary students can subscribe or unsubscribe whenever life requires them to do so. They can pick up their studies where they left off, giving them flexibility to devote time to family or church. We are committed to doing everything we can to ensure that we deliver high quality and value at pennies on the dollar compared to the average university. *One of our convictions is that time and money shouldn't be a barrier to someone's desire to know the Bible more deeply.*

TheosU and Theos Seminary are pioneering a path forward for the church and for higher education. We hope to one day see thousands of educated ministers of the gospel, proclaiming the message of Jesus in the world. We have been very blessed to see the response that we have and are grateful to our students for that.

If you have never experienced TheosU or Theos Seminary, we invite you to check us out. Subscribe to TheosU or apply to Theos Seminary. We would be honored to have you as a part of our community, as we are just getting started. We seek to model the innovation that we have come to admire in Harvard University with how we impact education. We hope to honor the continued legacy of John Wesley with how we serve the church. And finally, we hope to serve believers everywhere through accessible theology.

We know that the path forward is not quick or easy, but it is worth it. There is no greater cause than the education of a kingdom person for the purposes of God's business.

3

RECOVERING DOGMA

GABRIEL FINOCHIO

Not that I remember many things from my youth (nor that I remember many things in my life), but one of the things I do remember is that I discovered Rob Bell like a patriot discovers a traitor. I had always been taught to understand the battle between the church and the world, the flesh and the devil, but I had not yet understood the much more subtle battle between the church and herself.

All of my most up-to-date friends were reading Bell and Brian McLaren, but while McLaren always struck me like a nice grandfather, Bell was something more like a spell. His intellectual influence spread like music through a room full of eager listeners. Every book he released was like a hit single, and every film he presented was the music video that accompanied it. Bell represented the tip of the spear in what was called the emergent movement, which was simply a prelude to what we now call woke Christianity.

But I remember the moment I stopped reading Bell. It happened to be when I first started. I had finally bought one of his books and, after reading two chapters, I made the easy decision to close the book and hurl it into the garbage with all the force of God casting Satan out of heaven like lightning. What inspired this furious reaction was a curious passage I had come across in which Bell said that truth was like a trampoline and such trifles as the virgin birth and the Trinity of God were not meant to be stones but springs. They were not meant to be rigid, unbending, and inflexible, but things we play with, like toys, the amusements of children.

Well, all I can say is that when I became a man, I put away childish things like trampolines. (See 1 Corinthians 13:11.) I don't deny that doctrine is meant to be fun; I think it is. I think it's great fun to love orthodoxy. It's also great fun to fight heresy. But the point is that mankind has always enjoyed both war and peace because mankind enjoys being alive, and being alive can be both perilous and an adventure. But what strikes me as the whole hypocrisy of Bell's theology, if you could call it that, is that he prefers trampolines for the orthodox and castles for himself. The modern heretic attacks the castle of orthodoxy with the spring of the catapult and hides behind the safe brick walls of his own heretical castle. Every heretic has his own religion, which is the whole point of being a heretic.

The central mistake that modern heresiarchs make is in the assumption that by denying something, they aren't also affirming something. To continue the trampoline analogy, we can quibble about whether the heretic uses bricks or not, but he must at least admit he uses steel. A trampoline, after all, isn't composed of air. But regardless of the materials used, it is useless to pretend that the modern heretic isn't composing his own alternative religion. It's naive to think that because the heretic says something is wrong, he isn't saying something else is right.

G. K. Chesterton once wrote, "In truth there are only two kinds of people; those who accept dogmas and know it, and those who accept dogmas and don't know it."[1] The truth is that the modern heretic is a dogmatist as much as the most ardent Trinitarian. And one need only survey social media and the professional skeptics at universities everywhere to see that the heretic is much more dogmatic than the Christian. The sheer repetition of denial and the high-pitched screams of denunciation indicate little else than the fact that the heretic is much more interested in dogmatic heresy than the Christian is in dogmatic orthodoxy.

---

1. G. K. Chesterton, *Fancies Versus Fads* (London: Methuen & Co. Ltd., 1923).

Now, it has been part of the slow but happy discovery of my life as a Christian (and as a Chestertonian) that being dogmatic is a good thing. I confess I have gradually realized over the four decades of my life and over the painful process of thought that I am dogmatic and pugnaciously so. I'm afraid I have come to the conclusion that I hold a number of Christian doctrines so firmly that I would rather die than deny them. And not only that, but I think the only way to destroy the dogmas of heresy is with the dogmas of orthodoxy. I happen to think the spirit of Elijah that confronts the false doctrines of woke theology and deconstruction is the manliest and most biblical way to destroy them.

The word *dogma* comes to us, not from Latin, but from the Greek *dokei*, which simply means "it seems good." In that sense, dogma is not something forced on us, but rather something we force on ourselves. A dogma is an idea that a man holds as true. Even if someone says, "I don't believe dogma is true," he is stating, in a contradictory way, his dogma. In other words, there is no way around dogma. We may run away from certitude, if we like, but there is no escaping the fact that accepting ideas as true is part of the nature of reality.

Rocks have no dogmas, but then again, rocks are still somewhat dogmatic. The point is that everyone starts thinking at some point, and that point becomes their dogma, or they wouldn't start thinking at all. If a man starts thinking by accepting the idea that reality exists—a very good place to start—then he is what we call sane. If he moves from that sane dogma to another, such as the fact that reality is moral, with duties and rights, we call him a good citizen. If he grows into holding the more mystical but no less self-evident dogmas of love and the existence of God and the soul, he simply becomes even more ordinary.

A man holds a dogma, then, when he accepts his idea as true. The question isn't whether a man is dogmatic or not, but what he is dogmatic about. Everyone is a dogmatist. Some are simply dogmatic and wrong; others are dogmatic and right. We are all dogmatists because all of us intellectually accept that something is true, that something is real, even if that something is merely our egos.

Christian dogma, therefore, accepts the tradition of Christian truth. It accepts the doctrine that the Bible is inspired, inerrant, and infallible. It accepts the doctrine of the Holy Trinity, the virgin birth, the atonement of sin, Christ's dual nature, and the final judgment and hell. The modern Christian accepts these things as the ancient Christian once did and for the same reason. The early church was built by dogma, with each dogma acting as a stone, slowly forming the house of God. The church fathers rejected the dogma of Arius by accepting the Nicene Creed. They rejected the dogma of Apollinaris by accepting the Constantinopolitan Creed. They rejected the dogma of Nestorius by accepting the Ephesian Creed. They rejected the dogma of Eutyches by accepting the Chalcedonian Creed.

In each case, the orthodox church bravely chose to accept truth and define doctrine into rigid and precise stones, with each one used to form a new aspect in the structure of the church. The ancient church answered the deconstructionists of its day with simple yet profound construction. The heretics tried to take away the stones in the house of God, but the church fathers continued to build as the Holy Spirit led them.

The truth is that the church fathers were following the example set by the apostles, who were following the example set by Christ Himself. If the statements of Christ cannot be called dogmatic, then I don't know what He was trying to do. If He wasn't speaking in absolutes, then His messages are meaningless. What was the point of telling His followers *"I am the way, and the truth, and the life"* (John 14:6)? Christ's sermons would be pointless if they are simply seen as giving a personal opinion. Even ordinary people noticed that Jesus spoke *"as one who had authority"* (Matthew 7:29; see also Mark 1:27). Christ did not speak as a skeptic or a cynic, but as a dogmatist. He commanded and rebuked and counseled and warned as one who could not be contradicted and as one who could not be questioned.

In our time of decay and doubt, we have lost sight of the truth that Christ made dogma before He made disciples. We speak in tired tones about how "Christianity is a relationship" rather than a religion, but Christ offered religion before He offered relationship. The call of Christ was a dogmatic appeal to forsake all and follow Him. (See Luke 14:33.) It was upon that unbending basis that His followers became disciples. To say that Christ did not form a religion is to deny that His teaching had authority. The word *religion* comes from the same Latin word as *obligation*. It means restraint. And that is why it is universally condemned by the modern world—because it is a restraint and a check upon the godlessness and lawlessness of our age.

The modern world, being hopelessly humanistic, is centered upon the self, and the religion of Christ confronts our selfishness by obliging us to accept what He taught and what He willed, as opposed to what *we* want and will. But there is no discipleship without dogma. A person cannot be a disciple of Christ without accepting what He taught. We must accept the religion of Christ in order to have relationship with Christ. We must accept the building of the church in order to enter into it. We must accept orthodox Christian doctrine in order to be Christians.

The main mark of every epistle in Scripture, from Romans to Revelation, is dogmatism. When Paul, James, Peter, John, and Jude wrote, they wrote chiefly as dogmatists, as men with conviction and conclusion. They wrote emphatically as stones and not springs, and they were following the lead of the chief cornerstone, who is Christ. (See Ephesians 2:20.) They wrote to communicate the will of God to the people of God. And it is our responsibility to accept what they wrote. In that way, the Bible becomes our dogma when we accept what it says.

In contrast to this truth, it is almost the main mark of modern liberal churches that they do not teach the Scriptures dogmatically; that is, they do not teach their people to accept what the Bible says. The Scriptures were written by the church to be accepted by the church. Paul wrote, *"All Scripture is inspired by God and is profitable for teaching, for reproof, for correction, and for instruction in righteousness"* (2 Timothy 3:16 MEV). The Bible is meant to completely change our lives, but it can't change us if we don't accept it as dogma.

We hear much talk about biblical literacy these days, but it isn't good enough to simply know the Scriptures. The devil knows the Scriptures. We must *believe* the Scriptures and obey them. We must firmly accept them as our authority on faith and morals. And yet many of our churches treat the Scriptures as advice rather than as an authority.

If we treated God's Word as an authority, we would make it a priority. Our messages would be saturated with Scripture, rather than personal anecdotes, secular quotations, and catchy phrases. We neglect to accept the Scriptures as an authority and wonder why our people never grow into spiritual maturity. Do we believe what the Scriptures say about divorce and remarriage? Do we believe what they say about lust and homosexuality? Do we believe what they say about procreation and femininity? Do we believe what they say about holiness and hell? Do we believe what they say about repentance and regeneration?

The truth is that dogma is meant to come from authority, and when the average Christian does not accept the authority of Scripture, they will seek and follow other authorities. They will rely upon the authority of psychology, or science, or economics, or society, or the state. But those authorities are not divine; they are rooted in man rather than God. They offer not authority but tyranny. And today, the dogma of the state has replaced the dogma of the Scripture. Caesar has become God. We are told to accept the immoral orders of our society because "it's the law of the land," but the Christian has a higher authority than the state, and therefore another dogma that claims a higher loyalty.

The state may tell us to accept new gender pronouns, gay marriage, unlawful divorce, or abortion, but the true Christian cannot accept those immoral orders because he has already accepted the moral order of God. The dogma of Christian orthodoxy is the only rebellion against the dogma of the secular heresies. When the medieval church formed dogma upon dogma and anathema upon anathema, it was not, as many foolish Christians think, creating a tyranny over mankind. It was creating a freedom over Christendom. It was rebellion against the anarchy of the Dark Ages. It was obeying the command of God to subdue nature, rather than let nature subdue mankind.

The barbarians of the Dark Ages were the skeptics and cynics of their day. They refused to believe in the moral order and in the right of God's will over man's. The heathen hordes that sacked and pillaged the civilization of Christian Rome believed in the dogma of chaos, the law of the jungle. It was the Christian church alone that saved civilization from suicide by lifting its head and heart to believe in the dogma of order and the law of God. The medieval church may have suffered from complexity, but it certainly didn't suffer from confusion. We look back and examine each of those medieval Catholic stones of dogma with hypercriticism and prejudicial disdain, but we rarely step back and realize that the church was building something as glorious as a Gothic cathedral. It was attempting to build *"living stones"* into *"a spiritual house"* (1 Peter 2:5) of God by integrating the paradoxical dogmas of Scripture. It was trying to create a civilization that was simultaneously transcendent, triumphant, and militant.

We denounce that time as backward and benighted, but it was actually the only thing that saved Christian civilization from the backward slide of Islamic barbarism and the darkness of heathen tribalism. Do you really think it is an accident that the permanent image of warring righteousness in the fairy tales impressed upon children's minds is that of a medieval knight in shining armor? Whatever else the medieval church was, it was a fighting church, and it conquered the world.

But the church must recover its fighting spirit if it is going to recover its cultural inheritance. If there is no church militant, there will be no church triumphant. By its very nature, dogma is defiant and defensive. It refuses to give up territory to the enemy. The dogmatist defends belief; the skeptic defeats belief. Many Christians assume spiritual warfare is a thing of prayer, charismatic utterance, and houses full of crosses and icons, but while those things may certainly help, the true weapon of spiritual warfare is concentrated in one thing: the Word of God. In other words, dogma is the sword of the Spirit.

What did Christ use to defend Himself from demonic attack in the wilderness? Dogma. He told the devil, *"It is written…"* (Matthew 4:4, 7, 10). What did Paul use when he wrote against the false Corinthian apostles? Dogma. He said:

> *For the weapons of our warfare are not of the flesh but have divine power to destroy strongholds. We destroy arguments and every lofty opinion raised against the knowledge of God, and take every thought captive to obey Christ.* (2 Corinthians 10:4–5)

It is no accident that the only weapon listed in the armor of God is *"the sword of the Spirit, which is the word of God"* (Ephesians 6:17). It is by the Word that we wage war. And that sword has a double edge (see Hebrews 4:12), which points to the two purposes of dogma: to teach and to correct. (See 2 Timothy 3:16.) With one side, we destroy the false doctrines of the enemy; with the other, we promote the true doctrines of Christ. But either way, the blade is made of steel. It is made of strength and firmness. In that sense, we need men who will *"fight the good fight of the faith"* (1 Timothy 6:12); men who will *"contend for the faith"* (Jude 1:3); and men who know how to use the sword of the Spirit, which is why biblical training is so important.

The task of the church militant is to train swordsmen. It is to train Christians in the knowledge of God and His Word. But today, we have reduced our church experience to emotional rather than intellectual stimulation. The modern trendy church is trying to be transformed by the renewing of its emotions, rather than the renewing of its mind. Instead of plainly teaching the Word of God, we give slick emotional speeches that strike the average parishioner as more of a sales pitch than a sermon. Instead of teaching sound doctrine, our churches heap up for themselves teachers who tell the people what they want to hear. Instead of training Christians how to use the sword of the Spirit in the battle against the world, the flesh, and the devil, our woke leaders teach Christians to concede spiritual territory and compromise their faith.

The Reformation wars of religion are over, and the modern wars of irreligion have only begun. And even though there still may not be reconciliation between the Protestant and the Catholic, I would still prefer a society where the Calvinist and the Catholic continue to argue with the red-hot passion of conviction than the social swamp of secularists, humanists, and hedonists who want to silence argument altogether. The godlessness around us doesn't care about our family feud; it only cares about the fact that we are Christians. In that sense, J. R. R. Tolkien may have been writing prophecy rather than fantasy when he spoke into the future and saw Mordor on the march, attempting to destroy all that we love and hold dear.

What we need now is not a unity between orcs and men, dwarves and elves, but a unity between Baptists, Lutherans, charismatics, Presbyterians, Catholics, and evangelical Christians. The United States Declaration of Independence became dogmatic and therefore defiant when it announced, "We hold these truths to be self-evident…" If any man wishes to know how to start a revolution, let him simply say, "I hold these truths." Every dogma births a revolution. As good political philosophers, America's founding fathers knew that if they wanted their republican constitutional documents to stand the test of time, they must be written with the words of eternity; that is, they must be written dogmatically. And as the dogmas of the American Revolution helped to inspire a revolt against political tyranny, the dogmas of historic Christian orthodoxy must help the church to revolt against the godless militant secularism of our modern era.

Do you want to stem the tide of doubt? Be dogmatic about doctrine. Do you want to end the rot of moral compromise in the church? Be dogmatic about holiness. Do you want to fight the onslaught of societal breakdown? Be dogmatic about the family. Do you want to save your neighbor from hell? Be dogmatic about Christianity.

As Chesterton prophetically said at the dawn of our last disastrous century:

> The great march of mental destruction will go on. Everything will be denied. Everything will become a creed. It is a reasonable position to deny the stones in the street; it will be a religious dogma to assert them. It is a rational thesis that we are all in a dream; it will be a mystical sanity to say that we are all awake. Fires will be kindled to testify that two and two make four. Swords will be drawn to prove that leaves are green in summer. We shall be left defending, not only the incredible virtues and sanities of human life, but something more incredible still—this huge impossible universe which stares us in the face. We shall fight for visible prodigies as if they were invisible. We shall look on the impossible grass and the skies with a strange courage. We shall be of those who have seen and yet have believed.[2]

---

2. G. K. Chesterton, *Heretics* (New Kensington, PA: Whitaker House, 2013), 191.

4

RECOVERING THE GOSPEL

THOMAS WEST

Imagine you needed money to get home from a baseball game. You spent all your cash on the nachos with fake cheese, and your credit card is maxed out. You ask a random stranger for some cash, and they give you $15 to cover your ride home. How would you feel? You'd be grateful. Someone met one of your needs and gave you money.

Imagine that you've fallen into bigger trouble. You don't have enough money to cover your cable and Internet bill, which is three months overdue. It's serious. You get one of those letters where they threaten to switch off your services if you don't send them the money in the next couple of weeks. You panic. You reach out to your mega-rich grandmother, who generously gives you $150 to pay the bill. How would you feel? You'd feel great! You might even send her a card or FaceTime her to express your gratitude. Someone gave you $150 that you didn't have.

Imagine you've gotten into serious trouble this time. You need $1,500 to pay off your debt to a loan shark. You call this grandmother back again, and amazingly, she gives you $1,500 to pay for your stupidity. You'd be ecstatic! You'd take her out for a nice lunch at Chick-fil-A. More than posting a photo in your *stories* on Instagram to show your appreciation, this one gets on the *grid* #GrandmaSavesLives.

Imagine with me that you needed money to buy a house, and your grandmother gave you hundreds of thousands of dollars. You'd be blown away. You'd be tempted to fall down and worship her.

The size of the gift is proportionate to the love that you feel for the person.

Now imagine if you actually weren't your grandmother's favorite person. Imagine that you were actually her next-door neighbor and her greatest pain in life. You were actually her enemy. You stole from her. You mistreated and abused her. You spat in her face. Imagine she gave *you* that money anyway. That would be overwhelming kindness. Who on earth would love a person like this? No one would!

Except God...

This is a picture of the grace of the gospel. God's grace is God's generosity poured out on undeserving people. Grace is God's kindness shown to His enemies.

Salvation is not wages for work, a reward for attendance, a prize for achievement, or a bonus for good results. Salvation is God's free gift to undeserving people. This is the gospel.

This gospel ought to be absolutely central in our lives and churches. Everything ought to flow from the fact of the gospel and the realities that the gospel secures and brings about, but every issue is not a gospel issue. D. A. Carson wonderfully reasons this through in a *Themelios* article.[1] The gospel is not the ABCs of the Christian faith that you learn first before moving on to more complex and urgent teaching; the gospel is the A to Z of the Christian faith. The gospel is not a diving board from which we leap into the pool of Christianity; the gospel is the pool that we constantly swim around in and enjoy. Saint Jerome reportedly once said, "The Scriptures are shallow enough for a babe to come and drink without fear of drowning

---

1. D. A. Carson, "What Are Gospel Issues?," www.thegospelcoalition.org/themelios/article/what-are-gospel-issues.

and deep enough for a theologian to swim in without ever touching the bottom."

The gospel is urgently important and if we are going to be obsessive about anything, then we ought to be obsessive about the gospel. Speaking of the gospel, Martin Luther once said we ought to know it well, "teach it unto others, and beat it into their heads continually."[2]

This chapter covers what the gospel is and why it needs to be recovered.

THE GOSPEL

Gospel is an old word that means "good story."

When a king defeated an enemy in a foreign territory, a messenger would run ahead of the king into the newly conquered tribes and towns that were under a new regime, whether they knew it or not, and call out, "The king has conquered! Come now as welcome subjects under his rule… or else." The messenger would herald the news of victory, proclaim that good news, and invite people into the new reign and rule. The messenger would proclaim the gospel.

Christianity has *the* gospel, the good news. Among all the other tweets and headlines you read in a lifetime, only Christianity has *the* gospel. So what is the Christian gospel? What is the good news that Christianity is all about?

The gospel is like a beautiful diamond that must be examined from different angles to appreciate each and every facet. For our purposes here, we can look at the gospel through four distinct lenses: (1) the heart of the gospel; (2) the news of the gospel; (3) the story of the gospel; and (4) the goal of the gospel.

A lot of my thinking and framing has been shaped by my friend Trevin Wax, who first caught my attention when he was collecting gospel definitions on his blog.[3] He synthesized and developed those many definitions in his subsequent books. For a helpful summary of many gospel definitions and what it means to teach the gospel, read Wax's *Gospel-Centered*

---

2. Martin Luther, *St. Paul's Epistle to the Galatians* (Philadelphia: Smith, English & Co., 1860), 206.
3. www.thegospelcoalition.org/blogs/trevin-wax.

Teaching: Showing Christ in All the Scripture. To help you identify the true gospel amidst various fakes and frauds, read his earlier book, *Counterfeit Gospels: Rediscovering the Good News in a World of False Hope*.[4]

THE HEART OF THE GOSPEL

The gospel, in one word, is simply and beautifully *substitution*. There are some bloggers and a few theologians out there who will bristle and buck when the gospel is summarized in just one word. Of course, the gospel is so much more than this one word, but it is certainly not less.

Second Corinthians 5:21 is a wonderful summary of what we're talking about: God made Jesus Christ *"to be sin who knew no sin, so that in him we might become the righteousness of God."* God substituted Himself for undeserving and guilty sinners like me and you. The heart of the gospel, in a single word, is substitution.

THE NEWS OF THE GOSPEL

The heart of the gospel is contained in the news or the announcement of the gospel. It's the kingdom announcement that Jesus Christ is the promised Messiah who both lived and died in the place of undeserving and guilty sinners, rose triumphantly from the grave and began God's new creation, and now lives and reigns as King over the whole creation.

The announcement of the gospel calls for a response in the lives of people who hear it. The announcement elicits a response of repentance and faith. When you hear the news, you might wonder, *"What must I do to be saved?"* (Acts 16:30). The answer, repeatedly given all throughout the New Testament, is that we must both repent and believe the gospel. (See, for example, Mark 1:15; Luke 24:47; Acts 20:21; Romans 10:9.)

To repent means to make a U-turn. We repent of our sins—mourn over the crimes we've committed against God, turn around, and begin to move in the way of Jesus. We believe in Jesus Christ and trust in Him alone for salvation. We don't trust in Jesus plus good behavior, deeds, or works.

---

4. Trevin Wax, *Gospel-Centered Teaching: Showing Christ in All the Scripture* (Nashville, TN: B&H Publishing Group, 2013); and *Counterfeit Gospels: Rediscovering the Good News in a World of False Hope* (Chicago: Moody Publishers, 2011).

We trust in the finished work of Jesus Christ for us. This is the news of the gospel, and it is news that demands a response.

THE STORY OF THE GOSPEL

The news of the gospel will only really make sense when it's understood within the context of the story of the Scriptures. Imagine you somehow time-traveled back to the town square just moments before the town crier, the herald, arrived with a gospel. There you are, wearing jeans and a baggy flannel top over a fitted white T-shirt. The herald appears and announces, "Behold, the king beat the fool out of that other guy and has conquered. He's won it, so come into his kingdom." You are left wondering what this guy is up to with his life. Frankly, you don't know what to make of the news without some sort of context. There are too many missing pieces and details to really understand what is happening and how you should respond. You need the story to understand the news.

The Bible tells us the true story of the whole world—one big, beautiful drama, a grand narrative of cosmic redemption that is full of personal applications. As N. T. Wright says, "The whole point of Christianity is that it offers a story which is the story of the whole world. It is public truth."[5]

The Bible contains four plot movements:

1. Genesis 1 tells us the wonderful story of creation, in which God made the world and everything in it. In Genesis 2, the focus of the story narrows in on Adam and Eve and God's good intentions for their lives.

2. Tragically, the story takes a terrible turn in Genesis 3 when Adam and Eve break God's word and choose to live in God's world according to their own way. As a result of their sin, which was disobeying the word of God (don't eat from that one tree), all of creation was cursed and crashed into chaos. Graciously, God doesn't leave Adam and Eve in their sin but gives them a promise. In Genesis 3:15, God promises to send a Savior to crush the evil one and reverse the curse on creation.

---

5. N. T. Wright, *The New Testament and the People of God* (Minneapolis, MN: Fortress Press, 1996), 41–42.

3. Genesis 4 through Revelation 19 tells us the story of this drama of redemption. God gathered a group of people to be His special people, His prized possession. What made them unique would not be their resumes, background, church attendance, or lists of good works because none of that exists apart from grace. The whole world was filled with undeserving sinners. But God worked through Noah and Abraham to form a people called Israel. Through Israel, God taught His people about the necessity of a blood sacrifice for their sin and appointed prophets, priests, and kings to give us a glimpse and a flavor of who Jesus is.[6] God sent His own Son Jesus Christ, the promised deliverer from Genesis 3. He lived a perfect life, died in the place of undeserving sinners as their substitute, rose from the dead, and ascended into heaven. The Spirit of Christ was sent to help people see and remember Jesus today and lead the church of Jesus Christ.

4. Revelation 21–22 tells just some of how all of this is going to end. The best things we create in this world will be brought into the new heaven and new earth. God will be with His people, He will wipe away every tear from the pain and suffering that sin brought about, we will see His face, we will be His people, and He will be our God.

This is the story that helps make sense of the news of the gospel. Right at the center of it all is Jesus Christ. He is the very center of the gospel. *"For God so loved the world, that he gave his only Son, that whoever believes in him should not perish but have eternal life"* (John 3:16).

THE GOAL OF THE GOSPEL

The gospel births the church. The work of Jesus on the cross makes it possible for people to repent and believe and for the church to exist. In fact, the Bible actually tells us that it was the future vision of the church that kept Jesus Christ on the cross and enduring the suffering that sinners deserved. (See Hebrews 12:1–2.) That is powerful. On the cross, when Jesus was enduring the punishment for sin, He was looking forward to

---

6. I can't move through these ideas without recommending Christopher J. H. Wright's *The Mission of God: Unlocking the Bible's Grand Narrative* (Downers Grove, IL: InterVarsity Press, 2006).

His people, His blood-bought bride, who would be His prized possession. Francis Schaeffer argued rightly that Christians' relationships with each other constitute the criterion the world uses to judge whether their message is truthful, so the Christian community is the "final apologetic."[7]

The purpose of the gospel is to create a church to spread the news of Jesus Christ. In the Great Commission, Jesus said, *"Go therefore and make disciples of all nations, baptizing them in the name of the Father and of the Son and of the Holy Spirit, teaching them to observe all that I have commanded you"* (Matthew 28:19–20). Jesus sends His followers into all the earth with a mandate to spread His message. Followers of Jesus obey the gospel by living their life together in the church and fulfilling the Great Commission.

The tension and conflict of the world is only healed in the gospel. Christians are right to emphasize the need to believe the gospel, share the gospel, and preach the gospel, but we must also bear in mind that the implications of the gospel are both societal, sociological, and cosmic in scope. The French philosopher Jacques Ellul noted, "It is in receiving and in living the gospel that political, economic, and other questions can be solved."

GOSPEL RECOVERY

It may seem like I've spent a lot of time and detail explaining what the gospel is but it's essential to understand that before we can have a conversation about what the gospel is *not*. The gospel needs to be recovered from various perversions, misuses, and abuses. Here are just two.

RECOVERING THE GOSPEL FROM IDOLATROUS SUPPRESSION

Most urgently, the gospel needs to be recovered from our idolatrous suppression of it. Romans 1 teaches that God has revealed His character and attributes to the world in a general sense, which we call general revelation. This general revealing of the character of God is not enough to save someone because they must believe in the *special revelation* of Jesus Christ to be saved from their sins.

---

7. Francis Schaeffer, *The Mark of the Christian* (Downers Grove, IL: InterVarsity, 1977), 25; cf. Timothy George and John Woodbridge, *The Mark of Jesus: Loving in a Way the World Can See* (Chicago: Moody Publishers, 2005).

Chillingly, our hearts are so opposed to God that we do two things when we encounter the general revelation of God's character. First, we *suppress* the truth about God. (See Romans 1:18.) Like trying to hold a beach ball under water in the pool, we push the knowledge of God down and away, behaving as though it isn't true and He really isn't there. Second, we *substitute* or exchange the glory of our immortal God for other false gods. This is idolatry.[8] Romans 1:25 summarizes this idolatrous two-step: "*They exchanged the truth about God for a lie and worshiped and served the creature rather than the Creator, who is blessed forever! Amen.*" Everyone worships something—and if it's not God, it's wealth, power, beauty, intellect, or something else from this world.

The gospel must be recovered from idolatrous suppression. To help with this recovery, we need the clear preaching of the gospel in a general sense, studying of the gospel in small group and community gatherings, and personal meditation on the gospel and preaching it to our own hearts. When it comes to idols, it's not a question of *if* you struggle with worshipping something or someone else instead of God but *what* you struggle with worshipping in place of God.

Our idolatrous suppression of the gospel is beautifully summarized by John Stott:

> For the essence of sin is man substituting himself for God, while the essence of salvation is God substituting himself for man. Man asserts himself against God and puts himself where only God deserves to be; God sacrifices himself for man and puts himself where only man deserves to be.[9]

And so we return to the heart of the gospel: God graciously choosing to substitute Himself for undeserving sinners.

---

8. To develop strategies for engaging the suppress-and-substitute tactics that people employ in regard to God, I suggest Dan Strange's *Plugged In: Connecting Your Faith with What You Watch, Read, and Play* (Surry, UK: The Good Book Company, 2019).

9. John R. W. Stott, *The Cross of Christ* (Downers Grove, IL: InterVarsity Press, 2006), 188.

RECOVERING THE GOSPEL FROM CULTURAL CAPTIVITY

Lesslie Newbigin was an Englishman who studied at Cambridge and ended up in India as a foreign missionary for forty years. When he returned to England, he noticed that the church in Western culture was not living with missionary urgency and zeal like the church back in India. Upon further examination, he realized that the biblical story and the cultural story had blended together so much that it was nearly impossible to tell the difference between the two.

This blending of the biblical story and the cultural story is experienced in different ways around the world today. In the American South, to be American is also subconsciously understood as being Christian as well. The biblical story often gets dangerously blended into the cultural story that it is intended to transform. In a way, the gospel should always seem strange to us, but it never can be when it becomes domesticated within a particular cultural situation.

The gospel should live in a missionary relationship with the culture in which it is present. Its timeless message ought to be communicated afresh to every generation and in every cultural situation. In his own generation, Newbigin sought to bring about a "missionary encounter" between the gospel and the cultures in which he lived. First, he lived a life of faithful witness as an evangelist, pastor, and ministry organizer. Second, he developed a body of work aimed at equipping the church to bring about such encounters.[10]

The story of the gospel is the true story of the whole world and Christians are meant to immerse themselves in this story. The purpose of the gospel is to create a church for mission. Both the story and the purpose of the gospel can be recovered from cultural adaptation.

CONCLUSION

It is gracious to give someone something they don't deserve. Salvation is a gift that God graciously offers to the whole world.

---

10. Among other roles, Lesslie Newbigin was active in the World Council of Churches.

The goal of the gospel is to create a church for mission and worship, for the glory of God is the ultimate goal. We glorify God by being grateful for the grace that He shows to us, which is priceless.

Only the gospel will lead us to give God the glory He is due. Ray Ortlund said it best:

> The cross cancels all our debts. God says we're free to leave the past behind and move on with joyful relief. That is the mission of Jesus into your life. Will you welcome him?[11]

---

11. Raymond C. Ortlund Jr., *Isaiah: God Saves Sinners* (Wheaton, IL: Crossway, 2005), 409.

5

RECOVERING RECONCILIATION

STEPHEN WESLEY

When you first hear the word *reconciliation*, what flashes in your mind? A more theological mindset and worldview will evoke images that rarely arise in woke Western culture. Each day, the world and the church are confronted with concepts of reconciliation to the degree that we now have *truth and reconciliation commissions* to help governments try to heal the wounds of the past.

Reconciliation answers questions concerning righteousness, justice, forgiveness, mercy, and grace. Biblical reconciliation fully explores these truths when we grasp them theologically.

> So basic is this truth that without objective reconciliation there is no thought of salvation, of regeneration, of faith, of Christian life.[1]

Commenting on reconciliation in relation to Ephesians 2, the great church father Tertullian said, "He was born to reconcile both Gentile and

---
1. Walter A. Elwell and Barry J. Beitzel, "Reconciliation," *Baker Encyclopedia of the Bible* (Grand Rapids, MI: Baker Book House, 1988), 1824.

Jew to God, both of whom had offended God. He reconciled them into one body through the cross."[2]

Reconciliation was a twofold event. Reconciliation not only made us right with God, but it forged three separate entities into one. Christ, Jew, and gentile all became one through His flesh as He suffered on the cross.

What can I add to the reconciliation to make it complete? It started with God, and it was completed by God. You and I are the recipients of this reconciliation. Jew and gentile are now one in Christ Jesus.

The New Testament is filled with these astonishing new revelations. Jesus was the Jewish Messiah. Gentiles were uncircumcised and uncovenanted, not seen as having any part in the community of faith.

But the New Testament is rife with the realities of this new entity that has come about because God reconciled us to Himself and reconciled us to one another.

- Peter receives revelation not to call unclean what God calls clean. Right in front of him, God then saves and fills Italians with the Holy Spirit, which leads to a synod to understand what, in fact, God is doing. (See Acts 10–12 and 15.)
- Who is the true Israel? Both Jew and gentile in Christ. (See Galatians 6:16.)
- What is true circumcision? Circumcision of the heart, not the flesh. (See Galatians 5:5–6; Romans 3:29–30.)
- Paul rebukes Peter for his racial hypocrisy. (See Galatians 2:11–16.)
- *"God chose to make known how great among the Gentiles are the riches of the glory of this mystery, which is Christ in you, the hope of glory"* (Colossians 1:27).
- Do you have to fulfill the Mosaic law to be saved? No! (See Acts 15:19–21.)
- Abraham received the promise of faith while he was a gentile. (See Romans 4:3.)

---

2. Mark J. Edwards, *Galatians, Ephesians, Philippians: Ancient Christian Commentary on Scripture, New Testament VIII* (Downers Grove, IL: InterVarsity Press, 1999).

- Christ did away with the old classification system. (See Colossians 3:11.)

So how do we now have such varying ideas concerning reconciliation?

How reconciliation is lived out in our church experience may vary greatly depending on our theological anticipations of heaven. People of color and white evangelicals know there is a new wall of separation. Black Lives Matter, critical race theory, antiracism, and the ongoing cry for recognition provide evidence that the world is trying to answer pertinent needs and questions. I have felt the sting of racism, prejudice, and ignorance, so I know how powerful their poison can be. I lived with it pumping through my soul for many years. But those experiences cannot trump God's Word or His call on our lives, no matter our ethnicity.

In his book *How to Fight Racism*,[3] Jemar Tisby mentions reparations and estimates that African-Americans would be owed $40,000 to $60,000 per person to be adequately reimbursed for past injustices. Meanwhile, after reading the article "16 Bridge Building Tips for White People" from Be the Bridge (bethebridge.com), you must ask yourself if you would agree with the preconceived notions inherent in that document. If I disagree with your terms of how to be reconciled, where do I stand? Am I now unable to be reconciled or am I reconciled to you only by my works?

> *For he himself is our peace, who has made us both one and has broken down in his flesh the dividing wall of hostility by abolishing the law of commandments expressed in ordinances, that he might create in himself one new man in place of the two, so making peace, and might reconcile us both to God in one body through the cross, thereby killing the hostility.* (Ephesians 2:14–16)

As we saw earlier, the truth of reconciliation was only made possible to the Jews by direct revelation from God. They simply could not see it and had no heart or mind, no prayer or expectation whatsoever, for *"one new man in place of the two."* Yeshua was the Jewish Messiah. He was the king who had come to restore Jerusalem and Israel to the head of the nations.

---

3. Jemar Tisby, *How to Fight Racism: Courageous Christianity and the Journey Toward Racial Justice* (Grand Rapids, MI: Zondervan, 2021).

Peter's revelation in Acts 10 and the confirmation at the synod of Acts 15 only confirmed that God was doing something far greater while simultaneously fulfilling His promise to Abraham—namely that in Christ, all the families of the earth would be blessed.

These truths of reconciliation, oneness, and peace must be applied to the church of Jesus Christ in a restorative light, specifically to heal the relational gap that has transpired in the church through slavery and systemic racism. In the same way that Jews could not and did not consider gentiles their equals, many Christians had the same feelings toward Africans, and this was expressed in the mid-Atlantic slave trade.

Jesus is said to be our peace, our *shalom*, but when we hear this, we generally think of a cessation of conflict. But in the Hebrew and Middle Eastern worldview, it meant so much more. As theologian Cornelius Plantinga Jr. points out:

> The webbing together of God, humans, and all creation in justice, fulfillment, and delight is what the Hebrew prophets call shalom. We call it peace, but it means far more than mere peace of mind or a cease-fire between enemies. In the Bible, shalom means universal flourishing, wholeness, and delight—a rich situation in which natural needs are satisfied and natural gifts fruitfully employed, a reality that inspires joyful wonder as its Creator and Savior opens doors and welcomes the creatures in whom He delights. Shalom, in other words, it is the way things ought to be.[4]

The peace that Jesus made available on the cross created oneness for the Jew and the gentile and does so today for all ethnicities amid our history, wars, abuse, racism, and hatred. Christ enables us to be in relationship the way He originally intended.

Professor Miroslav Volf, the founding director of the Yale Center for Faith and Culture, writes that, indeed, reconciliation is multidimensional:

> Reconciliation between human beings is intrinsic to their reconciliation to God…Consequently, from the start, reconciliation does not simply have a vertical, but also a horizontal dimension.

---

4. Cornelius Plantinga Jr., *Not the Way It's Supposed to Be: A Breviary of Sin* (Grand Rapids, MI: William B. Eerdmans Publishing Co., 1995).

It contains a turn away from the enmity toward people, not just from enmity to God, and it contains the movement toward a community, precisely that community which was the target of enmity.[5]

Reconciliation is a spiritual condition, something that's true in the Spirit. From God's perspective, heaven's perspective, and a theological perspective, there isn't an African-American church, a white church, or an Asian church. What is true in heaven is true right now. We are one; we are reconciled. I am reconciled to you and you are reconciled to me because we are reconciled to Christ. Therefore, we are coheirs. Our skin color and ethnicity mean nothing; our faith means everything. Our faith says we're one. It's true whether we believe it or not.

I choose to believe it.

I'm not *trying* to get reconciled. I'm *living* reconciled. This takes grace.

As Volf points out:

> Though grace is unthinkable without justice, justice is subordinate to grace…At the core of the doctrine of reconciliation lies the belief that the *offer of reconciliation* is not based on justice done and the cause of enmity removed. Rather, the offer of reconciliation is a way of justifying the unjust and overcoming the opponent's enmity—not so as to condone their injustice and affirm their enmity but to open up the possibility of doing justice and living in peace whose ultimate shape is a community of love.[6]

The means to reconciliation is not justice, but grace and forgiveness. Jesus did this for us on the cross. He took God's punishment for sin and gave us grace and mercy, which we did not deserve. This is the stunning revelation of the greatness of God's love at work. But can this grand theological concept work in the nitty-gritty of everyday life and relationships, when injustice seems to thrive everywhere, and the world is replete with stories of systemic racism, tribalism, and religious intolerance? Can this be an answer to moving us toward the *community of love* we all know we need and want?

---

5. Miroslav Volf, "The Social Meaning of Reconciliation," *Occasional Papers on Religion in Eastern Europe*, vol. 18, issue 3, article 3; digitalcommons.georgefox.edu/ree/vol18/iss3/3.
6. Ibid.

John Calvin wrote, "If the Jews wish to have peace with God, they must have Christ as their mediator. But Christ will not be their peace in any other way than by making out of them and the gentiles one body. Therefore, unless the Jews admit the gentiles to fellowship, they have no connection with God."[7] This is revolutionary.

In the 1960s, civil rights leader Fred Hampton proclaimed that he was a revolutionary and urged others to make the same declaration. Well, King Jesus was the ultimate revolutionary and through His death on the cross, His message of reconciliation took people who were at war with one another for millennia and forged them into one. So powerful was the message of reconciliation that it ended any allowances for racism, prejudice, or ethnocentrism.

What about our churches today? If you're a guest preacher at a local church that's not multiethnic and multiracial, do you tell the congregation it has "no connection with God"? That's a surefire way to not be invited back.

But what is the *spirit* of the message of reconciliation? It's quite simple really. All are welcome, and none can be rejected, mistreated, maligned, or viewed as second-class or unclean. You are them and they are you—and until you figure that out, you are missing the central message of the power of the reconciliation that God has wrought in Christ.

How do we get there from here? I see two ways forward.

1. FORGIVING GRACE

Do we want justice…or do we want grace? Justice leaves little room for relationships and a community of love. Grace is far greater, for while justice has its place, in the Christian context, the sinless Son of God endured judgment so others could benefit and live in a relationship. Forgiveness does not sugarcoat or water down the need for judgment, but its desire for a relationship will endure suffering, offering forgiveness to one who does not even ask for it in order to have a relationship.

Inherent in humanity and God's order is the need for repentance for wrong actions. It is the mature and the wise who can acknowledge their sin

---

7. John Calvin, *Calvin's New Testament Commentaries*. Galatians through Colossians.

or the sins of their race or forefathers and honestly, for themselves, or on behalf of others, offer repentance. When this happens, hearts are softened, and relationships of understanding and intimacy can take place. Though I may never have agreed to or committed an atrocity of racial injustice, I can sympathize with those who have or those who have been marked by such pain.

However, revenge and reparations make matters worse. Volf explains:

Neither revenge nor reparations can redress old injustices without creating new ones. If you want justice and nothing but justice, you will inevitably get injustice. If you want justice without injustice, you must want love. A world of perfect justice is a world of love.[8]

Sin is a world issue. Throughout history, we have experienced wars based on racism, tribalism, and religion. If "perfect justice is a world of love," then how we heal to move forward is of paramount significance. Can you separate forgiveness from love? Forgiveness is the manifestation of true love, and reconciliation brings the transgressors home. It recognizes that the issue of reconciliation is an issue of the heart. Both the transgressor and the transgressed must determine in their hearts how they will now live for one another. When guilty, I will repent. When someone has sinned against me, I will forgive even as I have been forgiven.

Love—the fulfillment of the greatest commandments—is still the order of the day.

Like the father in the parable of the prodigal son, our heavenly Father is eager to welcome us back with open arms and reconcile us to Himself. But our hearts must be transformed. We must reinstate those seeking forgiveness. The church around the world is reconciled in the Spirit but still expresses itself along ethnic, tribal, and national lines. Specifically, in North America, the church is still separated along racial lines. Thankfully, a change is happening. For reconciliation to be fulfilled, it will be seen in how we love one another as new creatures in Christ and not out of the pain of our past. As Volf notes:

---

8. Miroslav Volf, *Exclusion and Embrace, Revised and Updated: A Theological Explanation of Identity, Otherness, and Reconciliation* (Nashville, TN: Abingdon Press, 2019).

> Much like Jews and Muslims, Christians can never be first of all Asians or Americans, Croatians, Russians, or Tutsis, and then Christians. At the very core of Christian identity lies an all-encompassing change of loyalty, from a given culture with its gods to the God of all cultures. A response to a call from that God entails rearrangement of a whole network of allegiances.[9]

My heart breaks every time I hear brothers and sisters being encouraged along racial lines not to attend a church of another race. There are too many stories of people being discouraged from loving or marrying outside of their race, though there is no scriptural mandate for this sinful practice of racial purity. When we love in transparency and vulnerability, the evidence of Christ's love will heal the brokenness that has come about because of the sins of our forefathers. My allegiances are to the Word of God and the truth of being a new creature in Him, which reveals itself in how I love my ethnically different brother or sister.

2. BELIEF IN OUR UNITY

Unity and oneness are the outworking of being reconciled. Jesus made it clear that when the world sees us as one, they will believe in Him. Sharing his thoughts on this essential unity, Volf writes:

> The Spirit unlatches the doors of my heart saying: "You are not only you; others are part of you too." No church in a given culture may isolate itself from other churches in other cultures, declaring itself sufficient to itself and to its own culture. Every church must be open to all other churches. Each church must therefore say, "I am not only I; all other churches, rooted in diverse cultures, are part of me too." Each needs all to be properly itself. In order to keep our allegiance to Jesus Christ pure, we need to nurture commitment to the multicultural community of Christian churches. We need to see ourselves and our own understanding of God's future with the eyes of Christians from other cultures, listen to voices of Christians from other cultures so as to make sure that the

---

9. Ibid.

voice of our culture has not drowned out the voice of Jesus Christ, "the one Word of God."[10]

The Antioch church of Acts 12 and 13 lived right in this very Spirit. The result was one of the greatest churches of the New Testament era, having an impact that lasted from the third century to the eighth century[11] due to its commitment to orthodoxy and orthopraxy. It was a church filled with the nations not just in its attendance, but in its leadership as well. They had a heart to hear what the Spirit was saying through the unique expressions of ethnicity within the church. They lived out reconciliation as Jew and gentile lived as one, and it produced a mighty generational church.

Today, evangelical churches seem to be leading the way when it comes to bringing different people groups together. Sociologist Michael O. Emerson says:

> The growing proportion of evangelical multiracial churches, I think, is the big story...It's more than tripled in these twenty years. By the way, as a sociologist who studies these things and watches how social change happens, there's no way ever I could have even imagined that would be possible; so it's the work of God.[12]

The truth of our oneness and reconciliation is becoming evident in the reality of church life. The cry to have a church that looks like heaven, filled with every nation, kindred, and tongue, is impacting pastors' hearts and how they envision church. The statistics bear witness to a move of God showcasing the oneness Jesus produced on the cross.

Living reconciled looks like fulfilling Jesus's commandment *"that you love one another as I have loved you"* (John 15:12). Jesus forged us into one, making us reconciled with God and one another. Our legacy is to live out His example and His love for one another.

God is watching, and the world is watching.

How will we showcase true reconciliation?

---

10. Ibid.
11. Walter A. Elwell and Barry J. Beitzel, "Antioch of Syria," *Baker Encyclopedia of the Bible* (Grand Rapids, MI: Baker Book House, 1988), 121.
12. "New Stats on Multiracial Churches," Mosaix Global Network newsletter, December 2019; accessed at multiethnic.church/released-new-2020-statistics-on-multiracial-churches.

6

RECOVERING APOCALYPTIC

CHRIS PALMER

These days, the term *apocalypse* comes with cold, miserable implications: doomsday…Armageddon…the end of the world.

How did apocalypticism get to this point? And can it be recovered so readers glean from it as much as they do from, say, Psalm 23?

I think so.

Before going further, it's important that I offer a definition. Apocalyptic is the literary genre of suffering people. It speaks into trying circumstances where God's goodness and sovereignty is placed into question.

Apocalyptic scholar Adela Y. Collins defines it as a literature genre "intended to interpret present, earthly circumstances in light of the supernatural world of the future, and to influence both the understanding and the behavior of the audience by means of divine authority."[1]

John J. Collins, another apocalyptic scholar, further defines it as:

---

1. Adela Y. Collins, *Early Christian Apocalypticism*. Semeia 36 (Missoula, MT: Scholars Press, 1987), 7.

A genre of revelatory literature with a narrative framework, in which a revelation is mediated by an otherworldly being to a human recipient, disclosing a transcendent reality which is both temporal, insofar as it envisages eschatological salvation, and spatial insofar as it involves another supernatural world.[2]

Using John Collins and Adela Y. Collins's definitions, the apocalyptic genre contains the following characteristics:

1. The elements of a story
2. Otherworldly beings who communicate with earthly beings to show them a different perspective
3. God's justice
4. Supernatural help that brings about God's divine, eschatological justice
5. Exhortation for how readers should live and respond to suffering and injustice

Naturally, we think of the book of Revelation. This is the only uniquely Christian apocalypse we have in our canon. In addition, the Old Testament contains Jewish apocalyptic. This includes the book of Daniel, as well as portions of Isaiah (24–27); Ezekiel (38–39); Joel (2:28–3:21); and Zechariah (1–6; 9–14).

There are other apocalyptic texts outside of our canon that are included in the pseudepigrapha.[3] Containing strikingly similar details to those in Revelation and Daniel, these writings are helpful for understanding Second Temple Judaism and early Christianity. These texts include 1 Enoch, 2 Enoch, 2 Baruch, 3 Baruch, 4 Ezra, and the Testament of Abraham.

Holocaust survivor Elie Wiesel, in his narrative of death camps, describes the kind of suffering that biblical apocalyptic readers would

---

2. John J. Collins (ed.), *Apocalypse: The Morphology of a Genre*. Semeia 14 (Missoula, MT: Scholars Press, 1979). His understanding of apocalyptic is based on the analysis of Jewish and Christian apocalyptic writings that come from 250 CE to 250 AD. See John J. Collins, "What is Apocalyptic Literature" in John J. Collins (ed.) *The Oxford Handbook of Apocalyptic Literature*, (Oxford, UK: Oxford University Press, 2014), 2.

3. The term "pseudepigrapha" means "falsely ascribed writings." These works, mostly written between 200 BC and AD 200, falsely claim to have been written by a key biblical figure. Though the authorship is forged, they are helpful texts that recount biblical narratives.

grasp. In the most chilling part of his graphic account, a young boy is being hanged. Wiesel walks past the innocent boy, pale and writhing, hovering between life and death. A fellow exclaims, "For God's sake, where is God?"

Horrendous evils place God on trial. Is He real? Maybe cruel? Or unjust?

The ancients wrote apocalyptic literature to tackle life-shattering questions of existence. Daniel instructs God's people on how to cope in exile. Revelation heartens those who find themselves facing social ostracization and persecution. First Enoch portrays a world of violence and injustice in which an unseen, heavenly realm operates to reverse injustice and bring salvation.[4]

The genre offers promises of God's intervention. This intervention often ends in the unprecedented age where God's justice satisfies the wails of the innocent, when His kingdom becomes all in all. Sufferers are exhorted to persevere and hold on to their confidence in God.

It is helpful in times of suffering.

Why, then, does apocalyptic cause today's evangelical church leaders to proceed with so much caution? Well, consider what apocalyptic has become known for: asteroids crashing into the earth, countdowns to doomsday, nuclear bombs exploding over cities, and complicated Bible codes.

How did apocalyptic go from being a genre that encourages and gives hope to one that terrifies and causes extremism? If we're being frank: dispensationalism.

Dispensationalism is a theological idea attributed to the nineteenth-century clergyman John Nelson Darby, an avowed Zionist. His teachings on dispensations produced a system of thinking about God's dealings with men, from the beginning to the end. They read like a master plan for all of history.[5]

These were organized into the Scofield Bible, published in 1909, written by C. I. Scofield. This study Bible added annotations to prophetic passages in the King James Version that followed Darby's eschatological

---
4. See George W. E. Nickelsburg, "The Apocalyptic Message of 1 Enoch 92-105," *The Catholic Biblical Quarterly*, 39.3 (1993), 309–328.
5. Barbara A. Rossing, *The Rapture Exposed: The Message of Hope in the Book of Revelation* (New York, NY: Basic Books, 2004), 23.

schemes—namely the doctrine of a premillennial rapture and God's dealings with national Israel.

Prophecy conferences, which were quickly on the rise, and the use of broadcast radio took advantage of Scofield's Bible, knitting Darby's master plan of how the world would end into the fabric of American evangelicalism *and* his system of the dispensations. The timing was ripe. By the 1920s and 1930s, the country had become rational[6] due to influences of modernity. Yet even before this point, theologians[7] had been well into allegorizing Scripture to explain away its supernaturalism. A plain, literal hermeneutic became a central way for the opponents of the higher critics to defend Scripture's supernaturalism. Darby and Scofield's system utilized this literal hermeneutic, and this made their system attractive.

This grassroots movement of dispensationalism intensified as the twentieth century rolled forward, leading up to the publication of Hal Lindsay's *The Late Great Planet Earth* (1970). Lindsay's book is significant in that it was the first to read the imagery in Revelation as twentieth century weaponry. Jerry B. Jenkins and Tim LaHaye's *Left Behind: A Novel of the Earth's Last Days* (1995) followed Lindsay's lead, updating its reading of apocalypticism to consider advances in weaponry and geopolitical significance.[8] Dispensationalism had achieved its height. The end of the world had become a riddle that could be solved by deciphering apocalyptic symbolism in light of current events, and Christ's return had become part of a global conspiracy.

Evangelicals alive today can attest that they have all grown up associating apocalyptic texts with recent conflicts in the Middle East, what's going on in Russia, the advent of a new pope, and any technological advancement that might make us all part of a one world government. Some of us have witnessed our parents buying survival kits to outlast the fallout of Y2K and even donating money to parachurch ministries dedicated to helping the nation of Israel rebuild their temple so Jesus can come sooner.

---

6. By rational, I am referring to rationalism: the idea that *reason* is the ultimate authority in religion.
7. The higher criticism of the nineteenth century allegorized much of the supernaturalism in Scripture, even going so far as to allegorize the resurrection. For a history of higher criticism in America, see Ira V. Brown, "The Higher Criticism Comes to America: 1880-1900," *Journal of the Presbyterian Historical Society* (1943-1961), 38.4 (December 1960), 193-212.
8. Rossing, *The Rapture Exposed*, 40.

Yet, dispensationalism simply does not provide faithful treatment of apocalyptic. Though the literal hermeneutic it employs did help to defeat the claims of the higher critics, it was also taken to such extremes within that scheme of dispensationalism that it did not leave enough room for loose ends, wonder, and the impact of actual allegory that *is* used in Scripture—all of which are natural to apocalyptic.[9]

So where does recovering apocalyptic begin?

The remainder of this essay will briefly touch on that.

The mystique of apocalyptic literature has always been the precise point that readers first misunderstand. John Christopher Thomas refers to it as its "fantastic imagery"[10] You know: flying scorpions, thrones that talk, animals that look like humans, and beasts that emerge from the mysterious sea. A misunderstanding of apocalyptic symbolism has enabled dispensational extremism and loads of poor interpretations that have resulted in disturbing consequences, to say the least. In recent times, misunderstanding apocalyptic symbolism led Charles Manson to commit his savage murders, caused David Koresh to start a malevolent cult that ended in tragedy, and gave Marshall Applewhite ideas that eventually lead to mass suicide.

The purpose of apocalypticism's fantastic imagery is not to give readers a riddle about the end of the world. Rather, it is to disorient the reader and shift the sufferer away from their earthly point of view, where there is pain and sorrow, and give them access to a heavenly perspective from which they can view their sorrows and suffering in order to hope in God.

Take 4 Ezra,[11] for example. This text is a Jewish apocalypse, composed in the late first century and addressing the suffering caused by the destruction of Jerusalem in AD 70. It is made up of seven visions that include all sorts of psychedelic imagery, such as a three-headed eagle with all kinds of wings, a talking lion, a weeping woman, and the Messiah who emerges from the heart of the sea. (See 4 Ezra 3:1–14:48.)

The visions begin by recounting Ezra's anxiety over questions pertaining to Israel's suffering:

---

9. Rossing, *The Rapture Exposed*, 25.
10. John Christopher Thomas, *The Apocalypse: A Literary and Theological Commentary* (Cleveland, TN: CPT Press, 2012), 14.
11. Chapters 4–13 in the Second Book of Esdras known as 4 Ezra.

> *I was troubled as I lay on my bed, and my thoughts welled up in my heart, because I saw the desolation of Zion and the wealth of those who lived in Babylon. My spirit was greatly agitated, and I began to speak anxious words to the Most High.* (2 Esdras 3:1–3)

Ezra enters the apocalyptic visions, and he becomes disoriented:

> *Then I woke up, and my body shuddered violently, and my soul was so troubled that it fainted. But the angel who had come and talked with me held me and strengthened me and set me on my feet.* (2 Esdras 5:14–15)

In this disoriented state, he loses earthly perspective. Soon, he sees Israel's sorrow and suffering from a heavenly perspective. His despair is turned to hope and confidence in God:

> *Then I got up and walked in the field, giving great glory and praise to the Most High for the wonders that he does from time to time, and because he governs the times and whatever things come to pass in their seasons.* (2 Esdras 13:57–58)

The fantastic imagery in 4 Ezra operates in the same way as the imagery in the apocalyptic text in our own canon. In Revelation 4:1–2, John enters a psychedelic vision that disorients him. This moves him from an earthly perspective as a sufferer on Patmos and shifts him to a heavenly perspective before the throne of God:

> *After this I looked, and behold, a door standing open in heaven! And the first voice, which I had heard speaking to me like a trumpet, said, "Come up here, and I will show you what must take place after this." At once I was in the Spirit, and behold, a **throne** stood in heaven, with one seated on the **throne**.*

(Dispensationalists understand this passage to be where the rapture takes place. This requires a stretch in reading the text because nothing is stated about the church being caught away in this passage…and yet *dispensationalists* are the ones who demand a "plain, literal" reading of the text.)

The position of this passage is significant. It comes immediately after Christ's last promise to those suffering in the seven churches (Revelation 3:21)—a promise that they will share His throne and join His reign:

*The one who conquers, I will grant him to sit with me on my **throne**, as I also conquered and sat down with my Father on his **throne**.*

In Revelation 4:1–2, John is standing before *that* throne.

The sufferer would understand that this throne is the eventual place from which they will rule with Christ (described further in Revelation 4–5). This would be immensely encouraging. It amounts to God's justice at work in their lives. Where is God? Ruling in their favor. He has invited them to be part of His reign. This heavenly viewpoint grants the reader a new, hopeful perspective.

Let's take a sample reading from another text.

In Revelation 18:1–24, readers find themselves approaching the end of the narrative, anticipating Christ's return. An angel reveals that Babylon has fallen and sings a funeral dirge. This signifies the final death and defeat of the world power that has been the oppressor of God's people:

Fallen, fallen is Babylon the great! She has become a dwelling place for demons, a haunt for every unclean spirit, a haunt for every unclean bird, a haunt for every unclean and detestable beast. (Verse 2)

In this song, the angel brings charges against Babylon for her sins. Then, he executes judgment on her (vv. 7–10). The world wails because of Babylon's defeat. Merchants can no longer become benefactors because of Babylon's demoralizing trade systems (vv. 11–19). An angel rises with a millstone and hurls it into the sea to illustrate the eternal defeat of this kingdom. Just as the stone will never rise again, neither will Babylon (v. 21). However, the people of God rejoice in her destruction and sing (19:1–8). This leads to the reign of Christ and eventually the coming of the new Jerusalem that replaces Babylon.

Since the time of the exile, Babylon has stood as imagery for the oppressors of God's people. In John's day, this would be the Roman Empire. Babylon (Rome) collapses. Injustices like cruel slave labor are overcome. The new kingdom arrives and isn't driven by greed. It doesn't build affluence by exploiting the innocent. Gone are those days. The righteous rejoice. The evil weep. Justice has come.

Doesn't seem complicated, does it?

We can glean contemporary application from both texts: the oppressive kingdoms and systems of this world will fall. Power structures that exploit the innocent will give way to the Godhead's fair rule. The sufferers who have been faithful to the Godhead will rule on the throne with the King of Kings. These two texts leave us with the impression that God is present and at work in our lives in *this* century. No need to dive into current events and contrive conspiratorial ideas around these passages. To haul out healthy applications for today, all it takes is a healthy treatment of the genre.

While pastoring through the mayhem of 2020, I relied on apocalyptic passages every Sunday. It's what kept our church disoriented—sane! The psychedelic imagery was our weekly break from the chaos of the news. We were seeing 2020 from a heavenly perspective. That included what Christ was doing to reconcile the world to Himself amid pandemic, injustice, violence, riots, and overwrought politics. A healthy treatment of apocalyptic is just what my congregation and I needed. I'm convinced we need more of it today.

To close, here are five practical ways to recover the power of apocalyptic. As Christian suffering upsurges, we would do well to purposefully make this genre part of our formation in Scripture:

1. ***Revise your reading.*** Begin your studies in apocalyptic text all over again. Start by reading primary sources. Daniel, Revelation, 1 Enoch, 2 Enoch, 4 Ezra, 2 Baruch, 3 Baruch, and the Testament of Abraham are good places to start. Dive into the historical situations of when these apocalypses were written. Examine the narrative features like the characters, the conflict, plot, setting, irony, and suspense. Find similarities in occasion, language, idioms, and symbolism. After familiarizing yourself with these primary sources, read secondary sources, like commentaries and Bible dictionaries, which will add to and aid what you've learned.

2. ***Build up and comfort.*** Remember, apocalyptic literature is intended to instruct God's people on how to respond to times of crisis and persecution. It's not a roadmap to the end of the world. It isn't conspiracy code. Approach apocalyptic with the intent to teach God's justice and unfailing faithfulness.

3. ***Avoid talking points.*** Follow where the text leads and avoid reading the talking points of your political affiliation into the text. Your interpretation should be guided by your growing knowledge of the apocalyptic genre. Don't let shock jocks, zealous pundits, and talking heads ruin your delicate analysis.

4. ***Present a faithful Christology.*** Daniel and the other apocalyptic portions of the Old Testament ultimately point to Christ, whom the book of Revelation is all about. (See Revelation 1:1.) This tells us that the way we present apocalyptic should be Christocentric. It must reflect a faithful Christology, and this includes the victory of Christ that was accomplished through His suffering. Christ is portrayed as a lamb (*arnion* in Greek) twenty-eight times in Revelation, which speaks of the suffering sacrifice of Himself through which He overcame. Jesus's paradoxical conquest over suffering, through suffering, shapes how we understand our own suffering in times of crisis and persecution, and leaves no room for escapism[12] or triumphalism.[13]

---

12. By escapism, I mean the notion that Christians need to escape the world and hurry on home to heaven. A pre-tribulation rapture is often criticized for being an escapist idea as it teaches that Christians will be removed from the planet before any real suffering begins. Escapism diminishes Christian responsibility in the here and now because, after all, "the whole earth is going to *hell in a handbasket* anyway." Escapism also overlooks the meaningfulness of Christian suffering and what God accomplishes through it.

13. Triumphalism is a theological framework that considers the glory of the Christian life without much, if any, regard for the suffering of the Christian life. Triumphalism diminishes the *already* and *not yet* tension of the kingdom of God in Scripture by focusing solely on the *already* facet. Like escapism, triumphalism also diminishes the meaningfulness of Christian suffering and what God accomplishes through it. Another term for triumphalism would be an *over-realized eschatology*. Defeatism is the opposite, since it focuses solely on the suffering of the Christian life without any regard for glory. Both triumphalism and defeatism are extremes. Gordon Fee calls for *realism* or a *radical middle* that doesn't expect too much or too little. See Gordon Fee, *God's Empowering Presence* (Grand Rapids, MI: Baker Academics, 1994), 9.

5. ***Let it lead to worship.*** The use of apocalyptic should end in worship. It's no mistake that apocalyptic texts offer some of the most explicit scenes of worship in all of biblical literature. Apocalyptic recounts the character of God and His just dealings with His creation. Knowing that God has foreordained His kingdom to overcome the horrendous evils and injustices in our world gives us reason to exalt the name of God and celebrate His victory. When we are using it correctly, it will lead to humble surrender before the One who sits on the throne of our lives.

There is a renaissance of apocalyptic literature among evangelical and Pentecostal Christians. Let us no longer allow dispensational extremism to make us timid about utilizing these texts. Rather, let's work at faithful interpretation of apocalyptic to preach the goodness and justice of God to those who suffer and need to hope in God again.

7

RECOVERING REVELATION

DAVID H. CAMPBELL

It's time to recover a biblical understanding of the last days.

A friend at seminary remarked, "Your eschatology affects everything you believe." At the time, I brushed off his comment. No longer. Here's why my view has changed.

The New Testament consistently asserts that all of God's promises to Abraham are fulfilled in Christ and His church, not in the state of Israel or the Jewish people. If you've watched the *Left Behind* series or listened to many popular preachers, you'll believe that the heart of God is focused primarily on the state of Israel. And if you believe that, you'll fail to understand the meaning of God's purposes for the church.

The New Testament consistently asserts that wars and political conflicts, famines, pestilence, and natural disasters will occur throughout the church age and are not in themselves signs of the end. If you believe the message that such phenomena are signs of the end, you will spend most of your time fixated on the latest news reports from the Middle East. You'll become fear-focused, not faith-focused, and you'll miss what God is really doing on the earth. You'll be like the lady who approached me after a seminar and said it was the first time she had ever heard teaching on Revelation that had left her with peace in her heart rather than fear.

The season of pandemic that we have recently passed through shows how this wrong thinking has dire effects in real life. Like me, you may have wondered why Christians seem to be suckers for the latest conspiracy theory. The reason is found in the *Left Behind* thinking, which tells us that the devil owns the world, and God has to resort to a rescue mission to remove the church before the enemy completely takes over. Those who believe this message will encourage you to see the activity of the Antichrist in every news report coming from Russia or the Middle East. The end is not only coming, it is practically here! That makes us, and more importantly, the gospel we represent, look foolish.

Have you ever wondered why the multitude of false predictions never come to pass? Think of predictions of blood-red moons portending a coming disaster as an example. Have you ever wondered why no one ever apologizes when they get it wrong, but instead make haste to move on to the next prediction? Have you ever wondered why the best-selling book *88 Reasons Why the Rapture Will Be in 1988*[1] was followed not by repentance, but by sequels with other predictions for 1993 and 1994?

I call this the eschatology industry. It makes a fortune for many who write books and speak at conferences, but it does nothing good for anyone else.

Do you see how your eschatology affects everything you believe and even how you live, even if you aren't aware of it?

Your eschatology definitely affects how you understand the Bible. For those of us who believe the Scriptures are the authoritative guide for faith and conduct, this is no insignificant matter. If we get the Bible wrong, we get everything wrong.

One of the best examples of how this happens involves our understanding of the Bible's last book, Revelation. The theological term for what I've been calling *Left Behind* thinking is dispensationalism. That view starts with the assumption that God has two separate covenant peoples, Jews and

---

1. Edgar C. Whisenant, *88 Reasons Why the Rapture Will Be in 1988* (Little Rock, AR: Whisenant/World Bible Society, 1988).

gentiles, and must fulfill His purposes for each. God sent Jesus to establish an earthly kingdom based in Jerusalem. Jesus failed to reach that goal, and so God created the church as a kind of Plan B. Dispensationalism teaches that God can only deal with one of His covenant peoples at a time, so in order to fulfill His original and most strategic intention, He must somehow get rid of the church and get back to His plan for Christ to initiate a Jewish earthly kingdom.

The vexing question for John Nelson Darby, the founder of dispensationalism, was how God was going to remove the church from the picture. He couldn't find any satisfactory solution in the Bible, and no one in all the history of the church had ever come up with a set of ideas like his. But then he struck oil. In 1830, Margaret MacDonald, a young woman in an early charismatic group called the Irvingites (which later wound up in heresy) experienced a vision in a prayer meeting in Scotland in which she seemed to see a secret return of Christ. Never had anyone, since the foundation of the church, taught such a doctrine.

But the idea of a *rapture* provided the answer for Darby, for it enabled him to remove the church and allow God to return to His starting point with the Jewish people. Darby quickly (and badly) reinterpreted a couple of Bible passages such as Matthew 24 and 1 Thessalonians 4 in a way no one had ever understood them to provide a biblical basis for the charismatic vision. And dispensationalism, as a system, was born. Elements of the system were quickly picked up by groups as divergent as Seventh-Day Adventists, Jehovah's Witnesses, and Mormons, though the connection is often poorly understood.

What dispensationalism teaches concerning Revelation is that, apart from the letters to the churches in chapters 2–3, the rest of the book deals with events of a final seven-year period of tribulation that takes place following the removal of the church from earth and the restoration of the state of Israel. Only the beginning and end of the book have any relevance for Christians.

One immediately wonders why God would conclude the Bible with such a book if it had little, if any, practical relevance for Christian believers. Darby's unconvincing answer, of course, was that God's concern is really for Israel, not the church. Granted, there is truth to be gleaned from the content of the letters to the churches, but that is a small part of Revelation as a whole. Further, it makes the letters look like a foreign piece of fabric artificially stitched on to the main body of the document, with no connection to the rest of it.

For these and many other reasons, I reject the dispensationalist interpretation of Revelation and the Bible as a whole. My contention is that wherever we misinterpret the Bible, there is a price to pay. That price includes failure to understand that part of the biblical message we got wrong, and the practical consequences for our walk with God and our daily practice of the Christian faith. If the Bible is our guide to life, getting it wrong will affect our lives in very down to earth and real ways.

Let's take this a step further. I believe that the true message of the book of Revelation has been seriously distorted—you could almost say hijacked—by the mistaken teachings of dispensationalism. That is a very serious matter, all the more so when we look at what I think are the three main things God wants to say to us through the Bible's last book. If Revelation is not a science-fiction novel dealing with a strange, post-rapture world, what does it really teach? There are three main points, all of which are critically important for us as followers of Jesus to understand.

1. THE WAY OF THE CROSS

Recovering the first message of Revelation: willingness to walk in the way of the cross and refusal to compromise is the path to eternal victory.

The letters to the seven churches lay out for us the challenges they are facing. The churches are pictured as being in a battle against an idolatry that has infiltrated some of the churches themselves. (See Revelation 2:14–15, 20–23.) The Roman emperor Diocletian demanded that people worship him as a god. The economy of the Roman province of Asia where the churches were located was organized into trade guilds. No matter what your occupation, you belonged to one of these. The Romans laid on the trade guilds one simple but (for Christians) devastating requirement: at certain appointed times, each guild had to gather to worship the emperor. If you refused to take part, the punishment was immediate ejection from the guild. That meant no work and no income in a society without any social welfare system. This explains the activity of the false prophet curtailing the ability to buy and sell (participate in the economy) for those bearing the seal of Christ rather than the mark of the beast. (See Revelation 13:16–17.) In other words, Christians as opposed to non-Christians.

To understand this theme of faithfulness in the face of persecution and temptation, it's helpful to realize that Revelation as a whole presents a replay of the exodus. Christians are pictured throughout the book as sojourners on their way out of spiritual Egypt, traversing a treacherous devil-controlled sea (12:15) through a wilderness full of temptations to idolatry yet also providing God's protection (12:14), on their way to the promised land of the new Jerusalem (21:1–22:5). During this journey, we will suffer at the hands of the enemy and his forces. Yet even as the cross and resurrection turned out to seal Christ's victory over Satan (5:5–14; 12:5, 7–11), so the present suffering of Christians seals our victory over the powers of darkness (7:13–17). Even while, like Christ, we suffer tribulation and hardship (1:9), we also share in Christ's kingly reign (1:6). In this present age, we may suffer physical hardship, but our spirits will be kept safe (11:1–12). The church's persecutors, on the other hand, will find themselves in the same position as Satan. Even as Satan's apparent victory at the cross triggered his ultimate defeat, so the present evil actions of unbelievers (11:10) are laying the basis for their final judgment (11:13, 18).

One of Revelation's main goals, therefore, is to exhort believers to remain faithful to Christ, in spite of present sufferings and the temptation to engage in idolatry represented by compromise with the world system. This faithfulness will eventually be rewarded in the heavenly kingdom. Notice that after the portrayal of the heavenly kingdom in 21:1–22:5, the final words of the book revert to the command to remain faithful. The heavenly visions serve as motivators for Christians now suffering in adversity to hold to the glorious promises of God and not fall away. Whatever we suffer now is worth it in light of the eternal reward we will receive.

Christians then and now should read Revelation and allow its portrayal of the divine majesty to motivate us to continued faithfulness. We are to live according to the values of this new world, not the world in which we live.

Understood as such, Revelation provides strength and comfort to countless Christians across the world today suffering under various degrees of persecution. Never before has the suffering of believers been so widespread and never before have so many died for their faith. Dispensationalism has robbed the suffering church of this comfort by turning Revelation into a science-fiction news report that has nothing to do with the church at all.

Revelation exhorts believers to stand fast in the face of adversity and refuse to compromise or give way to idolatry in light of our eternal hope. That includes you and me, trying to walk in faithfulness in the midst of enormous pressures to conform from a pagan, postmodern world. This message for all believers today is of vital importance for the health of the church. Don't allow misguided eschatology to rob you of it.

2. THE SOVEREIGNTY OF GOD

Recovering the second message of Revelation: the sovereignty of God in human history.

In chapters 4 and 5, John is given a vision of the heavenly court. The word *throne*, in relation to God, appears seventeen times in these two chapters. The vision thus expresses a strong statement about the sovereignty of God. In the vision, the Lamb is given a place of equal honor to God Himself, and the chapters as a whole portray the victory of both God and the Lamb. Because this vision serves as the introduction to all subsequent visions in the book, its focus is to demonstrate the authority of God and of Christ over all that is about to unfold. The trials of the believers who will also suffer from the effects of the various judgments upon the earth during the church age, the apparent triumph of the forces of the enemy, the eventual destruction of the latter, and the eschatological victory of the church are all under the sovereign control of God. God, not the devil, is in control!

Even the nefarious activities of the devil and his agents are in the end controlled by God. The Lamb opens the seals, assisted by the four living creatures (6:1–8), releasing demonic figures on the earth (6:2, 4, 5, 8). The angels release the trumpet judgments (8:2; 9:6–10:21; 11:15), during which God holds the key to the bottomless pit in which the demonic forces are released only under divine direction (9:1–6; 20:1–4, both passages referring to the church age). Godly angels release the bowl judgments (16:1–21), allowing the devil and his agents to send deceiving evil spirits throughout the unbelieving world (16:12–16). God is in control.

At the same time, the prophetic witness of the church, represented by the two witnesses of chapter 11, is equally under God's control. This includes their powerful testimony, their persecution and apparent death, and their eventual resurrection. Everything is under the hand of God.

It is therefore true to say that, according to Revelation, the hand of God is directly behind the tribulations of believers as well as those of unbelievers. The plagues in the book of Exodus, which for the most part struck Israelites and Egyptians alike, are used as a pattern for the trumpet and bowl plagues. But note that as in Egypt, believers have a measure of protection, signified by their sealing in chapter 7, which goes back to the blood of the Passover lamb. The mystery of why God would allow believers to suffer is answered throughout the book: God's strategy is to use their sufferings to refine their faith, while reserving unbelievers for ultimate punishment. As the heavenly court vision of chapters 4–5 leads into the initial unleashing of the divine judgments, it is clear that the resurrected Lamb is in control of all that is about to unfold (6:1). The kingdom rule of Christ is clearly pictured as released at His ascension, not during some hypothetical future millennium.

3. THE RESTORATION OF THE TEMPLE

Recovering the third message of Revelation: the restoration of the temple and God's presence.

Though we often don't realize it, the garden of Eden is presented in Scripture as the very first temple, and Adam is pictured as the very first priest. Why? Because God placed Adam in the garden to *"work it and keep it"* (Genesis 2:15). The same Hebrew verbs, translated as to "serve and guard," are used to describe the duty of priests and Levites in the tabernacle. They were to serve and guard it so nothing unclean entered the tabernacle. (See Numbers 3:5–10.) Adam's priestly duty was also to serve God in the garden as His vice-ruler and to guard against anything unclean entering it. In fact, he was commissioned to push out the boundaries of Eden to the ends of the earth. (See Genesis 1:28.)

We all believe that the story of the Bible is about the restoration of what was lost in Adam. In that case, we can expect the Bible to end with the restoration of the garden-temple. And that is exactly what Revelation presents, the only difference being that in the last garden-temple, the presence of evil is excluded.

We can trace the theme of God's temple all the way through the Bible. When Adam was expelled from the garden, God placed the cherubim to *"guard the way to the tree of life"* (Genesis 3:24). That is why statues of the same cherubim who guarded the entrance to the garden temple appear also on either side of the ark in the tabernacle (Exodus 25:18–22), and likewise in Solomon's temple (1 Kings 8:6–7). The tree of life reappears in the form of the lampstand—which in appearance was a flowering tree with seven branches—placed directly outside the most holy place in the tabernacle (Exodus 25:31–40). Solomon's temple was full of features that draw us back to the first temple in the garden: trees, gourds, flowers, pomegranates, lily blossoms, and so on. The presence of the cherubim symbolized the fact that access to this temple, while not forbidden entirely, was restricted to one man once a year.

Jesus pictured Himself as a new temple replacing the old physical structure (John 2:19). And then on Pentecost, the temple of God fell out of heaven and onto the city of Jerusalem. All God's people are incorporated by the Spirit into the new temple of Jesus. (See 1 Corinthians 3:16; Ephesians 2:19–22; 1 Peter 2:4–8.) This is why Christians are pictured as receiving the promise originally given to the Israelites of becoming a kingdom of priests and a holy nation (1 Peter 2:9), a theme that becomes explicit in Revelation (1:6; 5:10).

We would expect the Bible to end the way it began—in a temple. And so it does. (See Revelation 21:22.) Even as a river flowed out of the garden temple of Eden (Genesis 2:10), the temple in Revelation has rivers flowing out from the center (22:1–2). The tree of life is restored in the new Jerusalem (22:2). Even as precious metals were found in the garden (Genesis 2:12), so gold and onyx were prominent in the tabernacle and the temple (Exodus 28:17–20; 39:8–14), and reappear as gold, silver and precious stones in the temple of the church (1 Corinthians 3:12), and finally in the wall and foundations of the temple of Revelation (21:18–21). Even as the garden temple of Eden was on a mountain (Ezekiel 28:14–16), and Israel's temple was on Mount Zion, so also the end-times temple of Revelation is on a mountain (21:10).

The new Jerusalem is the fulfillment of God's plan to reestablish a garden-like paradise. Adam failed in his commission to extend the boundaries of the original garden. Israel likewise failed in her commission to be *"a light for the nations"* (Isaiah 49:6). But Christ succeeded where Adam and Israel failed. His Great Commission is a renewal of the original commission to Adam. The boundaries of the kingdom must extend throughout the earth by the end of the church age, which is why Jesus will not return until the kingdom has reached every nation. (See Matthew 24:14.) But in the new Jerusalem, the garden-temple is perfectly established forever. The serpent, allowed into the first garden, is cast out of the last garden. All God's expressions of covenant with men and women are fulfilled as they worship Him in the final, perfect temple.

To see Israel, from a dispensationalist perspective, as the ultimate inheritor of the promise of the kingdom and priesthood is to suggest that a rebuilt earthly temple is a greater fulfilment of God's plan than the church. This destroys the divine timeline of the loss and restoration of God's presence in His temple. To view Revelation primarily as a record of events in the Middle East after the church has been removed from the earth fatally distracts from its divinely-appointed place in the Bible. The last two chapters of the Bible complete the story begun in the first two, but they cannot be understood properly without seeing the line of fulfillment running through Christ and His church.

Let me leave you with a very sad story. Friends of ours were serving on the mission field in an Arabic-speaking country, where believers had correctly understood Revelation as a message to the suffering church and taken enormous comfort in that message. Unfortunately, some dispensationalist American missionaries showed up and told them the last book of the Bible had no words of comfort for them because it was all about God's divine intervention in creating the modern political state of Israel.

The blessing, they said, was for the state of Israel, not for believers suffering persecution for their faith in Christ. The impact on their faith was devastating.

Revelation is a book rich in theology, covering themes from protection in suffering to our security in God's sovereignty and on to the fulfillment of all that was lost in the garden.

What the *Left Behind* ideology has truly left behind is a poisoned well of unbiblical eschatology. That eschatology, if taken seriously, will blind us to seeing what God is saying to us in this last and vital book of the Bible, and how He wants us to live in light of Christ's return.

8

RECOVERING WORSHIP

LAYLA NAHAVANDI

As I sat down to write this chapter on recovering worship, my initial thought was, *How honest do we want to make this? How real am I going to be?*

My mind immediately flashed back to a night only a few months earlier. I was sitting at a conference with a preacher from another country, and we were both aware that yet another immorality scandal in the Christian worship movement was about to break. We sat in silence, heavyhearted over the state of the Christian worship industry and, I guess, more broadly, the state of holiness in the church in general.

Breaking the silence, my friend simply asked, "Where are the Keith Greens of our generation?"

Keith Green was a popular Christian worship leader and songwriter in the 1970s who died tragically in a plane crash at age twenty-eight. Known for songs like "Oh Lord, You're Beautiful" and "Create in Me a Clean Heart," he reminded one of John the Baptist in the way he called the church to repentance, holiness, and radical obedience to Christ.

After King David took Bathsheba to bed, there was one pathway forward, one road back to being the worshipper he was always meant to be:

repentance. In Psalm 51:10, David prayed, *"Create in me a clean heart, O God, and renew a right spirit within me."*

It's no secret that the Christian worship movement, particularly in the West, is in desperate need of a heart recalibration.

My first drafts of this chapter were sterile and academic as I danced around the topic, squeezing every drop of church history into my thoughts on worship, all the while hiding my face from the brutal reality of what really needed to be said.

You see, it just didn't suit my personality. I'm your happy-go-lucky Aussie Pentecostal preacher. I'm obsessed with Jesus and all things revival. How could I begin my chapter on worship with *this?*! Nah, that was for someone else.

But if we really want to recover worship, we need to be real. A recalibration must begin with recognizing where we are and moving toward where we need to be.

I'll leave a deeper discussion on where we are right now to those purehearted worship leaders and songwriters who are prophetically, graciously, and humbly leading the way. What I'd like to offer is a standard for recalibration.

Worship song has a long biblical history, with several passages mentioning practices such as psalm singing, hymn singing, prophetic songs, and singing in the spirit.

According to tradition, Saint Ignatius of Antioch is generally accepted as the first to introduce responsive singing into the more standardized practices of the church. It is said that he had a vision of the heavenly choir of angels singing praises unto God. Ignatius wrote:

> The psalm which occurred just now in the office blended all voices together, and caused one single fully harmonious chant to arise; young and old, rich and poor, women and men, slaves and free, all sang one single melody…All the inequalities of social life are here banished. Together we make up a single choir in perfect equality

of rights and of expression whereby earth imitates heaven. Such is the noble character of the Church.[1]

Saint Ambrose, the bishop of Milan, is known as the father of church hymnody. Ambrose referred to the Psalms as the "voice of the church." He recognized the presence of Christ in the Psalms and the power of worship for the persecuted church he led.

Ambrose is known for leading Saint Augustine to the Lord, and Augustine comments on the power of worship in Ambrose's congregation.[2] Augustine says, "For the singing of hymns and psalms...we have both the examples and the teachings of the Lord himself and of the apostles. In this practice, which is so useful for stirring the pious soul and inflaming the strength of divine love."[3] Furthermore, in his *Confessions*, Augustine writes:

> How did I weep, in Thy Hymns and Canticles, touched to the quick by the voices of Thy sweet-attuned Church! The voices flowed into mine ears, and the Truth distilled into my heart, whence the affections of my devotion overflowed, and tears ran down, and happy was I therein. Not long had the Church of Milan begun to use this kind of consolation and exhortation, the brethren zealously joining with harmony of voice and hearts.[4]

Augustine obviously believed in the power of worship music, although he also warned of the dangers of emotionalism. He and other church fathers were sure to differentiate their worship from the kind of Dionysian outpourings of passion that they associated with pagan culture.

Early Christians placed great value on congregational participation in worship.[5] Broad participation in the singing of psalms, hymns, and spiritual

---

1. Robert E. Webber, *Worship Old & New: A Biblical, Historical, and Practical Introduction* (Grand Rapids, MI: Zondervan, 1994).
2. Ibid.
3. Augustine, Letter 55.18.34 [Ad Januarium].
4. Augustine, *Confessions of St. Augustine Book IX Chapter VI & VII*.
5. Valeriy A. Alikin, *The Earliest History of the Christian Gathering: Origin, Development and Content of the Christian Gathering in the First to Third Centuries*. Supplements to Vigiliae Christianae, v. 102. (Boston, MA: Brill, 2010), 215.

songs is mentioned several times by multiple church fathers.[6] However, in the medieval church, worship music took a turn away from congregational participation. Webber writes:

> The value of medieval music is, of course, in its professionalism. The music is indeed beautiful and inspiring, but the fact that it was taken away from the people and put into the category of performance was undesirable for worship. Worship was no longer the action of the congregation; it was now the work of a privileged few.[7]

In an effort to avoid the spread of heretical beliefs through song, the medieval church overcorrected. In so doing, the church stripped the congregation of the beauty and transcendence of participation and limited the expression of worship in a negative way. However, the lesson we learn here is that theological accuracy in song is not optional. If worship through song is one of the ways we are to not only encounter God but also educate the church, then we must guard its theological quality. I will expand on this point in a bit.

After around a thousand years of congregational silence and restricted participation in the musical element of worship, the Reformers restored congregational singing. This represented a monumental shift in the trajectory of the church and a restoration of an aspect of worship that had been lost.[8] As an accomplished musician himself, it's no surprise that Martin Luther's influence on music in worship was revolutionary. Luther believed that music could be an incredibly powerful tool in spreading the gospel message. Webber notes Luther "also had the gift of writing and created music close to the hearts of the common people. His work was so effective that one of his enemies wrote, 'Luther's songs have damned more souls than all his books and speeches.'"[9]

The central focus of worship music in the church throughout history has overwhelmingly been placed on the singing of psalms. The ancient monastic movement centered on psalm singing, which was one of its most

---

6. Ibid., 219.
7. Webber, *Worship Old and New*, 238.
8. Ibid.
9. Ibid.

notable features. Medieval monastic music centered on psalmody, and the Protestant Reformation was known as a psalm-singing movement. Enormous effort went into producing vernacular, singable versions of psalms for Protestant communities. John Calvin worked with the composer Louis Bourgeois to produce a psalm book for Sunday worship.

In his *Letter to Marcellinus*, Saint Athanasius lays out a theology of psalmody, with special emphasis on the way the Psalms cover the whole range of human experience, to explain the centrality of psalm singing in the early desert monastic communities. Athanasius wrote:

> But we must not omit to explain the reason why words of this kind should be not merely said, but rendered with melody and song; for there are actually some simple folk among us who, though they believe the words to be inspired, yet think the reason for singing them is just to make them more pleasing to the ear! This is by no means so; Holy Scripture is not designed to tickle the aesthetic palate, and it is rather for the soul's own profit that the Psalms are sung. This is so chiefly for two reasons. In the first place, it is fitting that the sacred writings should praise God in poetry as well as prose, because the freer, less restricted form of verse, in which the Psalms, together with the Canticles and Odes, are cast, ensures that by them men should express their love to God with all the strength and power they possess. And, secondly, the reason lies in the unifying effect which chanting the Psalms has upon the singer. For to sing the Psalms demands such concentration of a man's whole being on them that, in doing it, his usual disharmony of mind and corresponding bodily confusion is resolved.[10]

Athanasius also spoke about the powerful effect that psalm singing could have on not only the singer but also the hearer, using the example of David ministering to the tormented King Saul through music.[11] (See 1 Samuel 16:23.)

In his longest work, the *Expositions of the Psalms*, a collection of sermons and sermon notes, Augustine develops his famous theology of *totus Christus* and the idea that Christ Himself is the ultimate psalm singer.

---
10. Athanasius, *Letter to Marcellinus*.
11. Ibid.

Therefore, all Christian psalm singing is really a participation in Christ's song. We unite our voice to His when we sing psalms. When the church gathers to sing, the corporate reality of Jesus is manifest.

In his *Prayerbook of the Bible*, Dietrich Bonhoeffer also argues that all the psalms give voice to Jesus's own experience and His own corporate reality. Bonhoeffer saw psalm singing as a central pillar to his monastic-style community of resistance in 1930s Germany.

The early church recognized congregational worship music as part of the proclamation of the Word. When the congregation sang, they proclaimed doctrine; thus, this music element of Christian worship was used as a way of educating the congregation. In addition to the Psalms, other Scriptures were proclaimed in song, recalling the crossing of the Red Sea (Exodus 15:1–18), the Song of Moses (Deuteronomy 32:1–43), and Mary's song of praise (Luke 1:46–55).

Worship music was used to spread both orthodox and heretical ideas. In the fourth century, Arius wrote songs popularizing his ideas that the Son was a creature of the Father. His writings and beliefs were condemned as heretical by several church councils. Since church buildings were forbidden to them in the capital city of Constantinople, on worship and festival days, the Arians would meet in public places, singing their songs antiphonally all night long. The tunes were catchy, and soon everyone was singing the songs, whether they believed Arius's doctrines or not.

Saint John Chrysostom, archbishop of Constantinople, feared this would draw people away from the truth, so with the sponsorship of Empress Eudoxia, he organized nightly processions and hymn singing with silver crosses, candles, and pageantry. At times, there were riots and bloodshed when the two sides met.

The early church viewed worship songs as more than just a convenient tool for indoctrination. They also placed a high importance on rational worship. There is a very close link in Christianity, as opposed, say, to the cult of Dionysus, between music and rationality. This is discussed in *The Spirit of the Liturgy*, the late Pope Benedict XVI's most influential book, published in 2000 when he was Cardinal Joseph Ratzinger. In it, Benedict says rational worship is a way of contemplating, grasping, and even feeling the truth of divine revelation. Worship songs have the power to generate an emotional response to rich rational content. In John 8:32, Jesus says, *"You will know the truth, and the truth will set you free."* Worship songs not only cultivate raw, indeterminate emotion but also the contemplation of divine truth. With this contemplation comes a deep witness in our spirit of life and freedom as we are transformed and conformed into the image of Christ.

The ancient church did not limit worship music to a cerebral proclamation of the Word of God or theological reflections. They also acknowledged the fact that worship music elicits an emotional connection and expression of one's relationship with God. As Paul tells us:

> *Hope does not put us to shame, because God's love has been poured into our hearts through the Holy Spirit who has been given to us.*
> (Romans 5:5)

This pouring out of the love of God into our hearts shows us that this experience is more than just a cerebral connection, more than just the knowledge that God loves us. It's also a heart connection. The Holy Spirit takes biblical and theological concepts and makes them experienced realties in our daily lives. Martin Luther said, "With all my heart I would extol the precious gift of God in the noble art of music…Music is to be praised as second only to the Word of God because by her all the emotions are swayed."

Early church historian Andrew McGowan states, "Music was a vehicle for the expression of the thoughts and feelings of ancient Christians as prayer and praise."[12] Similarly, Robert Webber, a theologian known for his work on early Christian worship and the ancient-future faith movement writes:

> Music also induces an attitude of worship. It elicits from deep within a person the sense of awe and mystery that accompanies a meeting with God. In this way music releases an inner, nonrational part of our being that mere words cannot set free to utter praise.[13]

---

12. Andrew Brian McGowan, *Ancient Christian Worship: Early Church Practices in Social, Historical, and Theological Perspective* (Grand Rapids, MI: Baker Academic, 2016), 111.
13. Webber, *Worship Old and New*, 233.

We are all aware of the power of music to reach deep into our souls and give us expression beyond the range of rational thought. Just think of what it can do when under the influence of the Holy Spirit!

Here are three ways we can recover worship and recalibrate ourselves to the beauty, purity, essence, and power of Christian worship in the ancient church.

1. LIFT YOUR EYES

Psalm 148 instructs all those in heaven and on earth to join in worship together. We need to remember that as we sing, we join in heaven's song. When we lift our eyes, we get our eyes off ourselves and our worldly pursuits, ambitions, and human-focused worship. When we lift our eyes, our worship naturally becomes centered on God because something more important grabs our attention.

You may have heard it said, "Don't be so heavenly minded that you're of no earthly good." I love how my pastor flips that on its head and replies, "Yes, and don't be so earthly minded that you're of no heavenly good." When we acknowledge that there is something transcendent about our worship and we shift our focus heavenward, we are beckoned into a deeper experience of the manifest presence of God here on earth.

2. TEACH WELL

We must recognize our opportunity and responsibility to shape the church's doctrine through song. We must commit to growing our understanding of doctrine and relationships that will help us facilitate that. A friend of mine who's an incredible songwriter at a large and influential church told me that whenever they write songs, they send the lyrics without music to the teaching pastor of their church to ensure the songs are doctrinally sound. What a great way to diligently steward their gift and responsibility with grace and humility!

Chrysostom, Augustine, and Luther highlighted the power of music to teach doctrine and pierce the human heart. We need not move away from pierced hearts. The answer is not to abandon worship music's emotional expression and engagement in a congregational setting. Instead, we should recognize the power of worship songs to both spread doctrine like wildfire and set hearts aflame with divine love for God when they are rooted in theological depth and biblical accuracy.

3. LIVE HOLY

Romans 12:1 (NIV) says, *"Therefore, I urge you, brothers and sisters, in view of God's mercy, to offer your bodies as a living sacrifice, holy and pleasing to God—this is your true and proper worship."* As worshippers, our first and most fundamental posture must be to present our bodies as a living sacrifice to God. We need to pursue purity, holiness, and repentance to allow the Holy Spirit to continue His work of sanctifying us daily.

So where are the Keith Greens of our generation? They're coming—and they will be a force to be reckoned with.

Who shall ascend the hill of the LORD? And who shall stand in his holy place? He who has clean hands and a pure heart. (Psalm 24:3–4)

9

RECOVERING THE SPIRIT

JOHN FINOCHIO

You've waded through the opening chapters of this book and perhaps are wondering whether you should even bother to read this chapter. Why would I say that? Because my experience has shown me that there are generally two camps within the twenty-first century church when it comes to pneumatology.

The first camp is fully decided upon what they believe and are not hungry or looking for more instruction when it comes to the Holy Spirit. It would be a mistake to assign that position only to those who are cessationist in their approach to pneumatology and not consider that there are those in the continualist persuasion whose beliefs are also settled. The second camp includes those who are either undecided or are decided but hungry to learn more and enter into a greater level of experience and understanding of the ministry and person of the Holy Spirit. I believe those in that second camp would profit the most from this chapter.

By now you're likely aware that TheosU is an advocate of a continualist position as it pertains to the gifts of the Holy Spirit, the baptism in the

Holy Spirit, and a church where these are not just talking points but a vital part of her ministry. Even so, perhaps you're wondering, *Did something happened to the Holy Spirit that He needs recovering?* Or maybe, *How does this jibe with the idea that the Holy Spirit was poured out on the awaiting disciples on the day of Pentecost and has been at work in the church since that time?*

Let's be honest here. Is the Spirit's work as robustly manifest as it was in the book of Acts and in other times of recorded church history? If not, perhaps that is where we need to start with recovery.

Although my cessationist friends would disagree, it is important to establish from the outset that there exists no clear irrefutable proof that the manifestations of the Spirit have ceased since the book of Acts.[1] Many reliable witnesses who have stood on both sides of this fence argue that the empirical evidence is that these gifts are as operational and available today as they were in the church at Corinth to whom the apostle Paul wrote. Those witnesses include a number of notable Christian leaders, many of whom were schooled in traditions that were cessationist, but, having since been exposed to these particular works of the Spirit, find it to be the equivalent of intellectual suicide to deny that these manifestations of the Spirit exist in the twenty-first century church.

In his book *Surprised by the Power of the Spirit*, Jack Deere writes:

> At first glance the reason for rejecting the gifts of the Spirit looks like a biblical argument but ultimately it is not. At best it is a confession of a lack of experience. The argument simply says that I do not see or hear of a contemporary ministry that has New Testament-quality miracles. But my limited experience cannot be used as proof that no such ministry exists today.[2]

The hang-up and bugaboo that our cessationist friends have about this really comes down to a desire to defend their tradition. Let's assume for a moment that is the case for some. Those who hold to cessationist traditions have known and associated with fine Christian men who instructed and taught them in seminary and in local churches and who did not give

---

1. See, for example, Thomas R. Schreiner, *Spiritual Gifts: What They Are and Why They Matter* (Nashville, TN: B&H Publishing Group, 2018).
2. Jack Deere, *Surprised by the Power of the Spirit* (Grand Rapids, MI: Zondervan Publishing, 1993), 58.

a moment's time to advancing any notions about these gifts being operational today. They seemed to get along just fine without them—or did they?

After Jesus had already commissioned His disciples to go and preach the gospel in all the world, didn't He say, "Do not leave Jerusalem until you have received the promise of the Father"? (See Acts 1:4.) Jesus certainly knew how ineffective and completely overwhelmed those early disciples would have been against the powers of darkness. Is it really any different today than it was then? Are we truly to believe that Jesus gave these dynamic gifts to one generation of the church and then vacuumed those gifts back up into heaven, where there exists no practical use for them or reason for them to exist, only to leave the greater balance of church history without the gifts and ill-equipped to face the challenges of gospel ministry that exist in every generation?

My own experience, the experience of thousands of pastors and leaders worldwide, and more importantly the Scriptures lead us to believe something entirely different and essentially vital to the work of the church on earth. As we proceed in this chapter, let's consider some dynamics that need to be recovered in the twenty-first century church.

DYNAMIC INFILLING

The book of Acts reveals that the entry point of the Holy Spirit's power upon the church was a powerful, dynamic one. There were rushing sounds of wind and tongues of fire appeared; the disciples began to speak in tongues—unknown languages of men and perhaps angels. (See Acts 2:1–4.) The Spirit from that point on seemed to be the one leading the parade forward, and it was His initiatives through the church that advanced the gospel, with mighty signs and wonders and gifts of the Holy Spirit following. (See Hebrews 2:3–4.) The change in these disciples could not be described as anything less than dramatic; many have pointed to the fact that the same disciples who fled and hid themselves in fear when Jesus was arrested, crucified, and buried were now bold as lions in proclaiming the resurrected Christ.

What accounted for such a dramatic change in such a short window of time? It was the dynamic infilling of the Holy Spirit. Every account of people being empowered by the Spirit in Acts and in Pentecostal and charismatic history is dynamic. It results in believers coming into an enduement of the Spirit's power to give witness to Christ, to live the overcoming Christian life, to minister in gifts of the Spirit, and to a glorious heavenly prayer language of their very own. (See 1 Corinthians 14:2, 14–15.)

Three tremendous nineteenth century revivalists also gave testimony of their own dynamic infilling of the Spirit.

First we have Charles Grandison Finney, whose ministry from 1820 to 1831 transformed entire communities and cities in New York State. Finney, a former lawyer, writes of his own experience after conversion:

> I returned to the front office [and] I received a mighty baptism of the Holy Ghost. Without any expectation of it, without ever having the thought in my mind that there was any such thing for me, without any recollection that I had ever heard the thing mentioned by any person in the world, the Holy Spirit descended upon me in a manner that seemed to go through me, body and soul. I could feel the impression, like a wave of electricity, going through and through me. Indeed it seemed to come in waves and waves of liquid love; for I could not express it in any other way…I wept aloud with joy and love…I literally bellowed out the unutterable gushings of my heart.[3]

When the first disciples received the gift of the Holy Spirit, Peter stood and preached Christ to the multitudes. Three thousand were saved and added to the church that day. (See Acts 2:41.) Finney's baptism in the Spirit made him so effective in evangelism that an estimated one hundred thousand people came to Christ in the city and region surrounding Rochester, New York. According to Finney researcher John Gresham, Finney continued to teach a baptism of the Holy Spirit subsequent to conversion and believed it to be universally proffered and available to all believers.[4]

---

3. Charles G. Finney, *Memoirs of Rev. Charles G. Finney*; online at www.gospeltruth.net/1868Memoirs/mem02.htm.
4. John L. Gresham Jr., *Charles G. Finney's Doctrine of the Baptism of the Holy Spirit* (Peabody, MA: Hendrickson Publishers, 1987), 12.

Dwight L. Moody, founder of Chicago's Moody Bible Institute, was another world-impacting evangelist with a strong belief in the baptism of the Holy Spirit subsequent to conversion. Moody believed the Holy Spirit could gift believers for service, saying:

> In some sense, and to some extent, the Holy Spirit dwells in every believer; but there is another gift, which may be called the gift of the Holy Spirit for service. This gift, it strikes me, is entirely distinct and separate from conversion and assurance. God has a great many children that have no power, and the reason is, they have not the gift of the Holy Ghost for service. God doesn't seem to work with them, and I believe it is because they have not sought this gift...We must pray for the Holy Spirit for service; pray that we may be anointed and qualified to do the work that God has for us to do.[5]

The third world-impacting evangelist of the late nineteenth and early twentieth century was R. A. Torrey. Known for powerful preaching and evangelism, Torrey was also a strong advocate for the baptism of the Holy Spirit as separate from conversion. He wrote and spoke frequently of this doctrine in his books and sermons. He explained:

> The Baptism with the Holy Spirit is the Spirit of God coming upon the believer, taking possession of his faculties, imparting to him gifts not naturally his own but which qualify him for the service to which God has called him.[6]

If you are one who has been taught or is teaching that we get all of the Spirit when we are born again and there is no need for a further dynamic infilling of the Spirit, I can only suggest that you look at the Scripture and see if this is so.

The baptism of the Holy Spirit came upon the disciples after they were already indwelled by the Spirit because Jesus breathed upon them. Just so, we are born of the Spirit at the moment of our salvation. However,

---

5. Rev. W. H. Daniels, *Moody: His Words, Work, and Workers* (New York: Nelson & Phillips, 1877), 396–397; accessed at catalog.hathitrust.org/Record/007114714.
6. R. A. Torrey, *The Baptism with the Holy Spirit* (Minneapolis, MN: Bethany House Publishers, 1972), 25–26.

that does not negate the need to be filled and baptized in the Holy Spirit. Perhaps in the church or tradition that you have come from, this wonderful aspect of the Holy Spirit needs to be recovered.

DYNAMIC GIFTS

What the cessationist and charismatic have in common is their belief in the work of the Holy Spirit soteriologically. This is important to acknowledge as it represents one of the most fundamental spheres of operation that Jesus ascribed to the Spirit of Truth. For both groups, this is acknowledged as being essential to the work of grace that leads people to repentance.

Speaking as a charismatic, I would agree that at times, it may appear that this is not given as much attention in charismatic churches as it merits. There is a temptation to sensationalize some aspects of the Spirit while not giving enough attention to the essential work of the Holy Spirit in convicting the world of sin, righteousness, and judgment. Admittedly, it would more likely be the case in charismatic circles to find people praying more assiduously for certain gifts of the Spirit to manifest than for the Spirit to be convicting and convincing sinners. It must also be recognized that the manifestations of the Spirit may be the means through which the Spirit does convict and convince an unbeliever as the apostle Paul states. (See 1 Corinthians 14:24–25.)

Pastor and author R. T. Kendall writes, "Theologically, I am on the side of those who adhere to the doctrine of grace in historic Calvinism. I am also on the side of those who believe the gifts of the Holy Spirit such as prophecy, healing, miracles and speaking in tongues."[7]

Kendall suggests what we need are churches that are committed both to gospel preaching and manifestations of the Spirit. He writes:

> I see a problem in churches I visit and preach in all over the world—imbalance. Churches are either committed to gospel preaching or desperately seeking visible manifestations of the Spirit. When I speak about Word churches, I mean the type of churches that emphasize preaching and getting doctrine right. Churches that

---

7. R. T. Kendall, *Prophetic Integrity: Aligning Our Words with God's Word* (Nashville, TN: Thomas Nelson, 2022), xxiii.

pursue healings, miracles, and other physical experiences I call Spirit churches…To find a church that adheres to solid theology, has consistent biblical preaching, sees regular conversions, and reports true miracles is rare.[8]

Notwithstanding, the second issue in the cessationist camp is that from a continualist perspective, they have not sufficiently entered into the things of the Holy Spirit. Protestant pastor and author John MacArthur has called some charismatic activity "strange fire," to which well-known charismatic leader Randy Clark wonders, "Is it a case of 'strange fire' or 'strangers to the fire'?" The apostle Paul thoroughly and enthusiastically endorsed speaking in tongues. (See 1 Corinthians 14:18.) Would it not simply be an act of humility to acknowledge one's lack of experience in gifts of the Spirit and leave it at that?

The fourth verse to Martin Luther's hymn "A Mighty Fortress Is Our God" contains these words:

> That Word above all earthly powers
> no thanks to them abideth;
> the Spirit and the gifts are ours
> through him who with us sideth.

My wife and I were ministering at camp meetings in Manitoba, Canada, when a young couple came for prayer as they had been trying for seven years to have a child with no results. We prayed and laid hands on them and sent them on their way. A few months later, I received a friend request from the woman; she was pregnant and wanted to inform me of the good news. It was a miracle! If not, it would have to be one incredible coincidence after seven years.

However, that is not the end of the story. Three years later, I was invited back to that church, where I began to minister in a prophetic manner as I felt directed by the Holy Spirit. This same young couple came forward with a three-year-old son in tow, asking if I remembered them. It was a joy to see the young miracle child and give him a hug. When I asked how I could pray for them, they admitted that they had been trying to conceive again without success. I closed my eyes. Silently within my own heart, I

---

8. Ibid., 34–35.

asked the Holy Spirit what He was saying to this couple. Immediately, the words, "Tell them they are going to conceive another baby" came into my spirit. I laid my hands on them and told them not to worry because the Lord is going to give them another child. A few months later, they were expecting. I thought, *This could get ridiculous if I have to travel there every time they want a baby!*

One recent Sunday, a woman told me that after I prayed for her healing from severe headaches the week prior, she bore witness that she was healed by the time she got to her car in the parking lot and had no headaches since. A young man on our worship team said he was experiencing lung issues that were similar to when he had COVID-19 a year previously. Someone gave a word of knowledge for that condition, and at the conclusion of the service, prayers were said for him. After a day or so, his lung issues were completely gone.

There are dynamic testimonies of God's work and miraculous answers to prayer that are experienced regularly in the Spirit-filled church that I feel are intended for the entire church world. We are not God's favorites, but being in an atmosphere where these requests for healing are approached in faith and being ministered to by those who are anointed by the Spirit is a game-changer. For that reason, I urge you, dear reader, not to become ambivalent about the Spirit's gifts but *"earnestly desire"* them, as the apostle exhorted the Corinthian church to do. (See 1 Corinthians 12:31.)

DYNAMIC FOCUS

The effectiveness of all churches could be dramatically increased—and their people better off—with a greater focus on the ministry of the Spirit. The Holy Spirit was given to the church for our profit. Jesus said, *"It is to your advantage that I go away, for if I do not go away, the Helper will not come to you"* (John 16:7). Everything that the Spirit of God does is good and profitable for the church. Every time a believer is filled with the Spirit, every time the Spirit releases His gifts—whether it be tongues for individual edification, prophecy for the corporate edification of a church gathering, healings, or words of wisdom—it always carries an impact that brings increase to the believer and to the church collectively.

The challenge lies in the fact that for God's people to become equipped to minister effectively in the Spirit requires focus. My experience tells me that most churches are not well suited or even positioned to bring a consistent focus to these things. Thus what is manifested is haphazard, immature, and at times dismal attempts to move in areas for which they have not been equipped. If we are really honest about it, we get what we focus on and we lack what we do not bring focus to.

As a pastor of twenty-three years and a minister-at-large in the body of Christ, I've found that I was welcomed into many churches based upon the gifts of the Holy Spirit that I had been trained to operate in, both by people and by the Spirit. This continues to be true to the present day. By the grace of God, I have been gifted and motivated to minister in these gifts. I covet them, yes, I *"earnestly desire"* the best gifts, especially that I may prophesy! (See 1 Corinthians 14:1.)

Jesus used spiritual gifts effectively in opening kingdom-of-God conversations and ministry to several people as recorded in the Gospels, such as the Samaritan woman at the well of Sychar, Zacchaeus, and Nathaniel. (See John 4; Luke 19:1–10; John 1:45–51.) Jesus gave words of wisdom to the rich young ruler, to those ready to stone the adulteress, and to Martha when she insisted that her sister Mary come and help her. (See Mark 10:17–22; John 8:3–11; Luke 10:38–42.)

I think these and many other manifestations of the Spirit in the New Testament created a dynamic of revealing the power of the kingdom that the church generally has lost and needs to recover. These are not things we create; our role is to cooperate with the mind and work of the Spirit in each ministry context. However, we must understand that the ministry gifts of the Spirit take many forms. We need to ask ourselves what we are losing when we fail to focus on what is given to us so graciously by Christ Himself through the bestowal of the Spirit.

DYNAMIC RECOVERY

In light of Paul's instructions in 1 Corinthians 14, we assume that the ministry and gifts of the Spirit are not meant to be esoteric. It makes no sense whatsoever to exhort believers to *"earnestly desire"* something that is not available to them. It is my conviction that everything about the Holy Spirit needs to be revered by the church in the twenty-first century. We should not come to this with complacent hearts for it would seem that we must approach the things of the Spirit with an earnest desire and expectation, thus Paul's exhortation.

Here are my recommendations to churches and people who desire to recover the fullness of the Spirit:

- **Preach/teach an in-depth series** on the person and work of the Spirit to build faith in your church.
- **Connect with leaders of integrity** whose ministry of the Spirit is well developed.
- **Personally pray and seek the Lord** for the baptism of the Holy Spirit inclusive of speaking in tongues, keeping in mind that all the early church leaders were tongues-talkers!
- **Establish a training ground** in your own local church. While it is great to bring in outside ministry from time to time, I have found that it can be powerfully effective to equip people in your own church in a team setting.
- **Pray and seek God earnestly** for the people of your church to be freshly filled with the Holy Spirit and provide a place and time where they can wait upon the Lord for this to occur.

10

RECOVERING OUR LANGUAGE

ELIJAH LAMB

When I started gaining a following on TikTok in 2019 for my awkward comedy videos, I didn't have a clue that within a few months, I would use the platform to talk to hundreds of thousands of people about the proof of God, the divinity of Jesus, and the Trinity. Now, the videos I was making certainly weren't pretty. They were weird, sixty-second clips of me talking into a mirror and zooming the camera every few seconds. Nonetheless, I was trying my best to teach theology to my peers through a quickly growing platform.

What I discovered early on was that nobody understood what I was talking about. This was puzzling. I didn't feel that I was being particularly confusing, so what was the issue?

The trouble, I gathered, was in the theological words I was using. It turns out that in a generation in which only 4 percent have a biblical worldview,[1] you cannot throw out a term like *hypostatic union* or *universalism* and

---

1. Jonathan Morrow, "Only 4 Percent of Gen Z Have a Biblical Worldview," *Impact 360 Institute*, 26 May 2020; www.impact360institute.org/articles/4-percent-gen-z-biblical-worldview.

be totally understood. My videos were always met with comments like, "I don't know any of these big words."

I recall a time when there was a debate of sorts among the other young creators on "Christian TikTok" regarding whether the app should be used as a place to discuss theology, or simply to preach the gospel. I remember hearing things along the lines of, "Theology is a distraction," "People only study theology because they're prideful," and "Deep theology confuses people, so it's not worth it."

I'm not sure the people who said those things believed any of that. More likely, they felt intimidated by the difficult, doctrinal talk they heard. I get why they responded the way they did. It's frustrating to know that what someone is saying is important and yet have no clue what any of it means because you're unfamiliar with the language they're using. It's like trying to join a conversation halfway through—you're missing key details that make your participation possible.

Every religion, worldview, philosophy, or general school of thought has "confessional language"[2] that makes understanding the perspective possible. Understanding critical race theory, for example, requires a knowledge of systemic oppression, white privilege, and antiracism. Understanding Freudian psychology requires a knowledge of the id, ego, and superego. Understanding Christianity requires a knowledge of the Trinity, salvation, and sin. Therefore, if I claim to be an adherent of any of these worldviews and yet do not have a clear understanding of their most essential terms, my beliefs become those of my own invention.

The problem of confessional language is where many cases of deconstruction actually lie, rather than theology. Deconstruction is best understood as the action that naturally follows the conclusion that narratives or beliefs that attempt to explain the world on a meta scale (religion, the scientific method, etc.) cannot be trusted. The goal of deconstruction is to break down the worldview you've been given by your community and come to understand all worldviews as being equally valuable…and none of them as being technically true. In this specific context, it looks like denying the fundamental beliefs that inform the Christian worldview and explaining

---

2. Willem F. Zuurdeeg, "The Nature of Theological Language," *The Journal of Religion* 40, no. 1 (1960): 1. www.jstor.org/stable/1200572.

them away as grabs for power and undesirable because of their claim to be an objective definition of reality.

The issue for many deconstructionists is not that they dislike Christian theology, but that: either the sources of their spiritual formation have given them definitions of our essential terminology that are inconsistent with their historical meanings; or they haven't been given the historical language of the faith at all.

So how did we get here? What has caused some churches today to retire the theological language that the church fathers worked so tirelessly to define, and in some cases, create? And how do we find, on a personal level, some kind of renaissance in our doctrinal talk?

Three things, I think, may be to blame:

1. Scientific ways of knowing
2. The seeker-sensitive movement
3. Post-structuralist thought

"Scientific ways of knowing" sounds complicated, but it really isn't. All that I mean by it is that in the West, we have been trained to think that we really can get to the bottom of anything that confuses us. There is nothing, we think, that can outdo our supreme intellect.

Today it seems that for something to be valid, it must make complete, scientific sense. Not that it must be correct, or even very smart, but it must be easily explainable.

The Scriptures, on the other hand, remind us that we only *"know in part"* (1 Corinthians 13:9) and cannot *"find out the deep things of God"* (Job 11:7). Much of what the Scriptures teach is drenched in "mystery." The kingdom of heaven (Matthew 13:11), God's will (Ephesians 1:9), the condition of Israel (Romans 11:25), the resurrection of the dead (1 Corinthians 15:51), the faith (1 Timothy 3:9), the gospel (Colossians 1:26), and Christ Himself (Colossians 2:2) are all described as such.

This means that the things we discuss in theology cannot be *fully* understood—a fact that generally tends to make the Western person uncomfortable.

The ancient theologians? Not so much. In an excerpt about describing or naming God, Thomas Aquinas wrote, "Whence a name is imposed, and what the name signifies are not always the same thing."[3] In other words, theologians can use words to try to describe God, but they won't always measure up—and that's okay. The church fathers seem content to do their best at making sense of God and His works that they knew would never *fully* make sense to them. And that is reflected in their use of language.

On the other hand, scientific kinds of thinkers often leave no room for paradox, mystery, or tension, and this is reflected in their language, as we will see.

So then, in a culture where mystery is hardly ever embraced, how is a seeker-sensitive church to respond? If Christian theology is going to be attractive, they presume, it has to be simple, uncomplicated, and unromantic. Thus, theology becomes minimalistic.

A few examples might help to clarify what I mean:

- How have we seen water baptism explained? Many churches have long abandoned the term *sacrament* because what is a *means of grace* anyway? Instead, we say it is "an outward sign of an inward change."
- How have we seen salvation explained? We don't hear much about us being snatched from the fire or made right before God. Instead, salvation is defined as the moment we "asked Jesus into our heart."
- How have we seen the atonement explained? Certainly, we cannot teach the dramatic, beautiful perspectives of Christ the Victor, penal substitution, or even ransom theory because they are unscientific. Instead, we've opted for just "At-One-Ment," defining this ancient concept with a four hundred-year-old etymology.
- Lastly, how have we seen the Trinity explained? Many of the recent teachings I have encountered online, for example, haven't sounded much like the Athanasian Creed. These are instead traded for analogies about the states of water, the parts of an egg, or the roles of a man.

---

3. St. Thomas Aquinas, *Summa Theologica*. Eighth Article [I, Q. 13, Art. 8].

Even further, much of the seeker-sensitive movement rides upon the wave of practicality. In my own experience, I felt it easy to grow more concerned with self-help and Christian living than being theologically and biblically literate.

I am not, of course, meaning to say that one is more important than the other. It is a serious matter for us Christians that we live as Jesus intends, that we be spiritually and emotionally healthy, that we have happy marriages, and that we are flourishing in every area of life. But theology cannot play in the background forever.

Orthodoxy (right belief) is no less important than orthopraxy (right living). Rather they are both nonnegotiables for our living in Christ. It is unfortunate then that much of what Christians consume today is strictly practical. In the West, your average churchgoer may never hear strong theological language, and even when they are, it's likely a quip or an easy saying that doesn't amount to much. A simplified theology is an open door for post-structuralism to swoop in and begin the process of deconstruction.

Post-structuralism is a specific field of postmodernism often having to do with words and their meanings. In *The Death of the Author*, Roland Barthes, a post-structuralist thinker, says:

> Writing is the destruction of every voice, of every point of origin. Writing is that neutral, composite, oblique space where our subject slips away, the negative where all identity is lost, starting with the very identity of the body writing.[4]

Barthes and his contemporaries like Jacques Derrida and Michel Foucault say meaning is really up to the spectator or interpreter—what the author intended doesn't really matter. There is no final meaning that anyone, including the originator, can decide. Derrida goes so far as to argue that words are not even an effective tool at explaining reality to begin with, thus the author's intended meaning cannot be ascertained.[5]

---

4. Roland Barthes, "The Death of the Author," *Image, Music, Text: Essays* (London: Fontana Press, 1990), 142.
5. Jacques Derrida, "Signature Event Context," *Margins of Philosophy* (University of Chicago Press, 1982), 329–30.

What happens when biblically illiterate Christians realize that they can't really explain any of their beliefs or define their most essential confessional language? Perhaps one of the greatest temptations will be that of deconstruction, which tells them that texts and words should be redefined as is convenient. Furthermore, a Christian who has not been taught the actual meanings of Christian language will have no trouble ignoring what the apostles or the early church fathers actually meant when they used it.

From what I can see, if pastors and teachers today do not clearly define our terms, the deconstructionists, who have much to say, will soon take their places as the most formative theological voices in the lives of believers.

- Where we have said that salvation is "asking Jesus into your heart," they have gone on and on about how it *only* means being freed to love as God intended.

- Where we have said that sin is *only* "missing the mark," they have gone on and on about how sin means only not doing good, charitable things and not loving yourself well.

- Where we have said that inspiration *only means* that the Bible is God's Word, they have gone on and on about how Paul and Jesus are in disagreement, and how the Scriptures are man-made, lost in translation, and have been changed to fit a narrative. To them, inspiration is just a silly idea.

Most of my personal interactions with these kinds of teachings have actually been on social media. Lots of folks have built entire platforms detailing their deconstruction *journeys* and citing beliefs like this as being especially formative to their current perspective on God and the church. It's no longer somewhat obscure liberal theologians promoting these thoughts; it's individuals with hundreds of thousands of followers, which unfortunately means that deconstruction is growing increasingly popular.

Hopefully, you can see the process. Because our education and upbringings are drenched in scientific thought, which tells us there is nothing we cannot know, we are unwilling to embrace mystery in theology. In order for the church to survive in a world like that and have its doctrines received, it must teach only what is practical and easily accessible—there can be no difficulty in making sense of who God is or what He's done. When Christians realize that this means they have nothing but empty phrases and words they can't define, they are prone to redefine them at will to something more culturally appealing, rather than something understood as being ancient.

So how do we stop this pattern? How do we as individuals recover the language of the church and in this way become theologically literate?

Naturally, I suppose, we must undo the three errors I've already covered.

This means that first, we must become willing to leave room for mystery in our thinking. If Gustaf Aulén was right when he said, "For theology lives and has its being in these combinations of seemingly incompatible opposites,"[6] then we truly must *"become like children"* (Matthew 18:3) if we want to benefit at all from the study of theology.

As Aquinas implied, language is a tool we use to describe God and His acts, so it will, in many ways, fall short. The historical language of the church, though often technical, is only an attempt at explaining the inexplicable. If we want to learn about such things that we only *"know in part"* we must be content with language that only reveals in part, which is much better than language that doesn't reveal at all.

A practical way to begin this journey is to fall in love with fantasy. A mind that is well acquainted with legend, fable, and myth will be more apt to embrace the doctrines we hold. This has been my strategy at least: to fill myself with fiction and verse. Now I feel that if God were not mysterious, I would be shocked.

Why is reading literature the best first step to childlikeness? As Northrop Frye explains, "Literature gives us an experience that stretches us vertically to the heights and depths of what the human mind can conceive, to what corresponds to the conceptions of heaven and hell in religion."[7]

Stretching your imagination will prepare you for the impossible beauties of Christian theology.

---

6. Gustaf Aulén, *Christus Victor: An Historical Study of the Three Main Types of the Idea of Atonement* (New York: Collier, 1986), 155.
7. Northrop Frye, "The Keys to Dreamland," *The Educated Imagination* (Bloomington, IN: Indiana University Press, 1964), 101.

Now then to the problem of our weakened definitions. If we are not being taught the language of the church fathers, we must take it upon ourselves to discover it.

Deconstruction often occurs because of a surface-level understanding. To avoid that issue, we have to ensure that our theological roots go deep, knowing that "deep roots are not reached by the frost."[8] When we do that, we will realize just how rich the language of the early church was.

Take, for example, a few of the words I mentioned earlier: *baptism*, *atonement*, and the *Trinity*. Let's see what the fathers have to say in comparison to our common, modern explanations.

They say baptism is "a resplendent garment, an unbreakable seal, a chariot to heaven, a royal protector,"[9] our "panoply"[10] or a splendid display, and it is where we are "enlightened."[11]

How does this compare to our *outward sign of an inward change?* The church fathers tell us that there is some incredible power and beauty in baptism that changes us, draws us nearer to heaven, and comforts us. They apply a mysterious power to that dunking into water or sprinkling that we have long forgotten. Obviously, our definition is not on par with the language they were using.

Furthermore, of the atonement, they say:

> The Redeemer came and the deceiver was overcome. What did our Redeemer do to our Captor? In payment for us He set the trap, His Cross, with His blood for bait…By shedding the blood of One who was not his debtor, he [Satan] was forced to release his debtors.[12]

> In this [Isaiah 53:3–8, the prophet] shows that Christ, being apart from all sin, will receive the sins of men on Himself. And therefore He will suffer the penalty of sinners, and will be pained on

---

8. J.R.R. Tolkien, "Chapter 10: Strider," *The Lord of the Rings: The Fellowship of the Ring* (Boston: Houghton Mifflin Co., 1954).
9. Basil the Great, *Sermons on Moral and Practical Subjects* 13:5, A.D. 379.
10. Ignatius of Antioch, *Letter to Polycarp* 6, A.D. 110.
11. Clement of Alexandria, *The Instructor of Children* 1:6:26:1, A.D. 191.
12. Augustine of Hippo, Sermon CXXX.

their behalf; and not on His own. And if He shall be wounded by the strokes of blasphemous words, this also will be the result of our sins. For He is weakened through our sins, so that we, when He had taken on Him our faults and the wounds of our wickedness, might be healed by His stripes. And this is the cause why the Sinless shall suffer among men.[13]

How do these statements fare next to "at-one-ment?" The fathers described Christ's wonderful atonement as a substitution or a taking of our place, as a trick in which God fooled the devil and as a ransom God paid to Satan, much like Aslan.[14] These are clearly much more descriptive, vivid understandings than we tend to hold today.

Lastly, of the Trinity, they say:

> The statements made regarding Father, Son, and Holy Spirit are to be understood as transcending all time, all ages, and all eternity. For it is the Trinity alone which exceeds the comprehension not only of temporal but even of eternal intelligence; while other things which are not included in it are to be measured by times and ages.[15]

> The unity is distributed in a Trinity. Placed in order, the three are the Father, Son, and Spirit. They are three, however, not in condition, but in degree; not in being, but in form; not in power, but in kind; of one being, however, and one condition and one power.[16]

> That we worship one God in Trinity, and Trinity in Unity,
> neither blending their persons
> nor dividing their essence.
> For the person of the Father is a distinct person,
> the person of the Son is another,
> and that of the Holy Spirit still another.
> But the divinity of the Father, Son, and Holy Spirit is one,

---

13. Eusebius of Caesarea, *Proof of the Gospel* (Demonstratio Evangelica), Book III, Ch. 2.
14. C. S. Lewis, *The Chronicles of Narnia: The Lion, the Witch and the Wardrobe* (New York: HarperCollins, 1983).
15. Origen of Alexandria, *On First Principles*, Book 4, Chapter 4, 1.
16. Tertullian, *Against Praxeas* 2, A.D. 216.

their glory equal, their majesty coeternal.[17]

On this very important subject of the Trinity, the fathers spent centuries creating and refining the language that they would use to describe the very nature of God. Unfortunately, some Christians have almost abandoned it altogether.

If we want to be a people who thrive theologically, it is important that when we say *baptism*, we mean what Christ and His earliest followers meant by it; that when we say *atonement*, we mean what the fathers meant by it as they were informed by thousands of years of Jewish tradition and the writings of the apostles; and that when we say *Trinity*, we do not mean a modalistic, Arian, or partialist view of God, but instead what the fathers meant when they nearly murdered one another trying to get it right. We have to forgo easy explanations and be discipled by the hard work of using and understanding proper doctrinal terminology.

This finally leads to the problem of post-structuralism. Fortunately, the solution here is easy: just be humble! It's easy to feel that you have the best explanations, ideas, and language of all time, but you don't. And neither do I. We're walking in someone else's footsteps—so in order to avoid the nasty route of deconstruction, we have to trust that whoever walked before us ended up where we want to be.

Rather than standing all alone on an ideological island of your own invention, join into the long legacy of Christians who have been seeking to know God rightly.

All this being said, I have hope that if my generation can put these three simple things into practice, the daunting horror of "big words" will be no more. I look forward to a future where my generation stands confidently on a deeply rooted foundation of rich theological language, a future where we all talk like monks, or something close.

Thought and language are to the artist instruments of an art.[18]

---

17. *The Athanasian Creed*, lines 4–11.
18. Oscar Wilde, "Preface," *The Picture of Dorian Gray*, in *Lippincott's Monthly Magazine*, July 1890.

11

RECOVERING HISTORY

JOSHUA BIEDEL

> Aside from teaching us about God, sin, and the need for redemption, a significant portion of the Old Testament recounts the history of the people of God. These are the narratives that constitute the memories of the Christian community. These memories inform our identity as Christians.
> —Bruce Waltke[1]

Today's humans are born on third base, yet we think we hit a triple. What remedy can rectify such cluelessness? History is her name, and she is the old friend you never knew you needed to know better on your pilgrimage.

Let us quickly dig into the diagnosis of why humans—and Christians too no doubt—have long been indifferent to history. The reasons are myriad. Yet two common culprits often cited for humans being allergic to history are ignorance and apathy. One is reminded of a youth who was

---

1. Bruce K. Waltke, *An Old Testament Theology: An Exegetical, Canonical, and Thematic Approach* (Grand Rapids, MI: Zondervan, 2007), 14.

asked which of those culprits is the primary reason, to which he memorably replied, "I don't know, and I don't care." A Gen Zer never spoke truer words (unbeknownst to him).

What is humanity's cost for abandoning history? Simply put, pride and unawareness, wallowing in the shallows (or third base, if you will).

More relevant is this question: what is the price of historical neglect by Christians? See above, for starters. Yet, moreover, that price is scarily enlarged because our stakes are higher. For it is not tasked to Buddhists, Muslims, Jews, or Confucianists to assist God in saving the world, but to followers of Jesus. Greater stakes equal greater responsibility.

Make no mistake, *a radical recovering of history is nonnegotiable for a robust Christianity*. Period. And the more robust our faith, the more the Great Commission is realized. For a believer, knowledge of world history is vital, but knowledge of Christian history is even more paramount. Coupling both the secular and the sacred creates layers of depth sorely needed inside our modern brains with their short attention spans.

In his seminal *Celebration of Discipline* some fifty years ago, pastor Richard Foster wrote, "The desperate need today is not for a greater number of intelligent people, or gifted people, but for deep people."[2] Christian reader, look for no further for solutions to depth than history; history's dividends are depth itself.

A necessary pause is warranted to provide a definition of history before we progress. History is the story of past peoples, places, and events…for the purpose of becoming better humans. Why that definition? In short, the world's stage has seen certain people in certain places, doing certain things that have influenced posterity for better or worse. And just ascertaining that triad of components—people, places, events—actually means nothing if there is no application. An additional step is needed. One must take that compelling information and transact it to adapt, modify, correct, and allow it to make one a better human—or, in our case, a better Christian.

The old don of Oxford himself, C. S. Lewis, encapsulates it best:

---

2. Richard Foster, *Celebration of Discipline: The Path to Spiritual Growth* (New York: HarperCollins, 1978).

Most of all, perhaps, we need intimate knowledge of the past. Not that the past has any magic about it, but because we cannot study the future, and yet need something to set against the present, to remind us that the basic assumptions have been quite different in different periods and that much which seems certain to the uneducated is merely fashion. A man who has lived in many places is not likely to be deceived by the local errors of his native village; the scholar has lived in many times and is therefore in some degree immune from the great cataract of nonsense that pours from the press and the microphone of his own age.[3]

Substitute the word "microphone" with "Internet and social media" and this piece catapults higher to resounding relevancy for us today. Don't even get me started on TikTok.

In other words, Lewis says woe to the man who refuses to travel to many places (the past) outside of their own native village (the present). Woe to the base runner who is standing on third base without realizing how his ancestors advanced him along the base paths prior to his existence.

Woe upon woe to the Christian standing at the cusp of two thousand years of church history with nary a clue of the creeds, councils, battles, schisms, theological developments, heresies, leaders, setbacks, progress, eras, agonies, and ecstasies that have led to this moment in God's providential oversight of Jesus's bride.

I press the point further. It is not enough to simply know history and use it to become a better human. None of us is naïve enough to believe that intellectual assent in reading an article in a compilation book by numerous TheosU staff about recovering this or that aspect of essential Christianity is a game changer. Transformation demands more. It is not enough to know how or why we stand on third base—we need to know how to head to home plate. This formula provides clarity:

History + Conviction + Compassion = Recovering Robust Christianity

---

3. C. S. Lewis, "Learning in War-Time," in *The Weight of Glory: And Other Addresses* (New York: HarperCollins, 1949, 2001), 58–9.

Conviction without compassion turns into coldhearted Puritanism; compassion without conviction slips into shoddy heresy. Bones, like convictions, are rigid, firm, and unyielding. Flesh, like compassion, is warm, welcoming, and flexible. Only both bones and flesh constitute a body; suffice it to say that the body I'm allegorizing now is history itself. And as of late, the body of history looks like an already emaciated Portland hipster on the fifth day of his juice fast, with his skinny jeans miraculously starting to sag, wondering why he has zero energy and isn't flourishing in life.

Yes, Christian reader advancing through this chapter, there are more subjects to study in your spiritual walk than just theology, doctrine, and all things Bible (sprinkled in with Dave Ramsey's Financial Peace University, of course).

Allow me to start with reputable secular sources to vouchsafe for the refuge of history before I marshal scholars and theologians alike, to be succeeded by copiously sprinkled doses of Bible for divine measure.

Cicero, the gleaming light of the fading Roman Republic, long reaped the benefits of history's treasures. As his country was ravenously unraveling during the civil wars, antiquity's preeminent statesman bemoaned, "No one knows thoroughly Roman history, from which as occasion demanded could summon as from the dead unimpeachable witnesses."[4]

The constellation of great men inevitably orbits the twin stars of conviction and compassion for history, never mind the history they made themselves.

Winston Churchill wrote award-winning histories. Alexander the Great slept with a copy of Homer's *The Iliad*, the poetic story of the Trojan War, history's greatest conflict before Alexander's time. Abraham Lincoln knew the stories of the ancient Greeks and Romans intimately. Napoleon incessantly devoured history treatises. Over a quarter of Shakespeare's plays were histories. Today, pastor and author Rick Warren duly divides his theology book readings into four categories of church history:

1. Birth of the church to the Reformation
2. Reformation era
3. The last one hundred years

---

4. Cicero, *Selected Political Speeches* (New York, NY: Penguin Classics, 1969).

4. Present day

Even the successive ancient Greek trinity of philosophers—Socrates, Plato, and Aristotle— well knew that their majestic subject of philosophy was actually masquerading as history. They espoused the view that *history is philosophy with examples.*

One may be forgiven for forgetting that the Bible is one contiguous story of history, proliferated with explicit (and implicit) history lessons; referential recaps of people, places, and events are legion. God evidently loves history; according to tradition, God tasked Moses not only with writing the Ten Commandments but also Genesis, Exodus, Leviticus, Numbers, and Deuteronomy, kick-starting the holy Scriptures. Yet we often do not love history because our antennas are so askew away from it. Thus the Bible seen as history may as well be a zebra camouflaged in tall grass—unnoticed, undetected, and undervalued.

Who can forget history's shortest teaching lesson, just three words expressed by the Son of God Himself: *"Remember Lot's wife"* (Luke 17:32).

A redneck fisherman of the ancient Mediterranean world fell back on the anvil of history to empower his epistle. Thus Peter wrote:

> *For if God did not spare angels when they sinned, but cast them into hell and committed them to chains of gloomy darkness to be kept until the judgment; if he did not spare the ancient world, but preserved Noah, a herald of righteousness, with seven others, when he brought a flood upon the world of the ungodly; if by turning the cities of Sodom and Gomorrah to ashes he condemned them to extinction, making them an example of what is going to happen to the ungodly; and if he rescued righteous Lot, greatly distressed by the sensual conduct of the wicked… then the Lord knows how to rescue the godly from trials, and to keep the unrighteous under punishment until the day of judgment, and especially those who indulge in the lust of defiling passion and despise authority.* (2 Peter 2:4–10)

An eye of acumen will note the list of historical situations that Peter summons, as they all build—as one brick laid upon another—to culminate in verses 9 and 10. (See Isaiah 14:12–15; Genesis 6–9; Genesis 19:1–29.)

Lest the readers lose track of the very point of such historical citations, Peter connects the dots for us with these principles:

- *"The Lord knows how to rescue the godly from trials, and to keep the unrighteous under punishment until the day of judgment"* (verse 9)
- *"Especially those who indulge in the lust of defiling passion and despise authority"* (verse 10)

Paul was the converse of Peter in that he was no uneducated country bumpkin. In fact, he was *"a Hebrew of Hebrews…a Pharisee"* (Philippians 3:5). Paul sensibly elevates history to its proper place: that of teacher and instructor. He writes to the church of Corinth:

> **For I do not want you to be unaware, brothers**, *that our fathers were all under the cloud, and all passed through the sea, and all were baptized into Moses in the cloud and in the sea, and all ate the same spiritual food, and all drank the same spiritual drink. For they drank from the spiritual Rock that followed them, and the Rock was Christ. Nevertheless, with most of them God was not pleased, for they were overthrown in the wilderness. Now these things took place as examples for us, that we might not desire evil as they did…We must not put Christ to the test, as some of them did and were destroyed by serpents, nor grumble, as some of them did and were destroyed by the Destroyer.* **Now these things happened to them as an example, but they were written down for our instruction**, *on whom the end of the ages has come. Therefore let anyone who thinks that he stands take heed lest he fall.*   (1 Corinthians 10:1–6, 9–12)

Is your conviction for history ascending yet? If Peter and Paul didn't do the trick, let's circle back again to Jesus, which every Sunday school kid knows is the right answer to everything. Jesus corroborates the study of history to recover any sense of what God is doing now and at any time on His earthen footstool. Take note of His repeated, exasperated reply to the Pharisees who forsook history: *"Have you not read?"* (Matthew 12:3) and *"Search the Scriptures"* (John 5:39). In layman's terms, Jesus scolded them for not knowing history. (I have a feeling He would have been an ultra hardcore history teacher who assigned massive amounts of homework and ten-page essays over the weekend; grace and mercy are fit for salvation, but not for Jesus's fourth period AP history class that drags your GPA down.)

Salvation history "is the backbone of the Old Testament," and as J. I. Packer once noted, "Spine trouble…limits what a person's other limbs can do."[5] If you do not know your biblical history, your spiritual limbs are limited. No wonder most celebrity pastors' sermons are one dimensional—they're stuck in one position, with spine trouble that has severely limited their spiritual limbs. They traffic in inspirational quips instead of the saturation of Scripture. No Scripture = no history = anemic sermons.

No offense: I would excitedly beat you over the head two hundred and forty times to instill a guaranteed appreciation for history, especially Christian history. Why this random number? (And no, I'm not an overly excited person, although my ex-girlfriends would disagree.) Because the New Testament writers quoted the Old Testament over two hundred and forty times. In other words, they constantly pulled back the curtain of the present to peer back at the past and all its nuggets of delectable wisdom. To them, history was a fond companion.

I will not leave you hanging without action steps, fine reader. We are all on the same page regarding the radical recovery of a robust Christian faith, are we not? But how?

In short, you must supplement your intellectual diet with heavy intakes of history. This alone will fuel a fledgling conviction for it, thus fertilizing seeds of compassion for history as well; these components coalesce. I won't lie to you, however: you must put in the laborious work for this to magically sprout so you can deftly answer the question, "How the hell did I end up on third base out of nowhere?!"

Allow this author, as a former public school history teacher for middle school through college and lay pastor in churches across three states, to propose a blueprint for you to help achieve this:

Step 1: Adopt a posture of humility.

Step 2: Revisit the Bible with fresh eyes.

Step 3: Gorge yourself on preeminent historians.

---

5. Waltke, *An Old Testament Theology*, 20.

Step 4: Continue to binge-watch all things Kardashian—just kidding!

Step 5: Acclimate yourself with church history.

First, humility is prerequisite for any endeavor, especially this one. Why? You cannot learn or appreciate new things with a sense of entitlement. Plotinus, a third century Greek-Roman philosopher who influenced Augustine, said, "To be in pursuit of something is to admit inferiority." To put it another way, you will not value your position on third base if you do not first humble yourself and acknowledge the pristine field, exquisite stadium, and the sound rules of the baseball game that all preceded you.

Second, with history more on your radar now, reread the Word with fresh expectations of identifying the prodigious times it pops up everywhere. Such frequency will astound you.

Third, here are three gentlemen to whet your twin (and likely nonexistent) appetites for conviction and compassion for history: **Tom Holland**, **Plutarch**, and **Thucydides**. Drink, imbibe, and add their historical astuteness to your diet of thought. Why these three? Both Plutarch and Thucydides are primary sources of history—they partook in history in ancient Greece, and their writing is history itself. *Plutarch's Lives*, featuring biographies of famous Greeks and Romans, and Thucydides's *History of the Peloponnesian War*, covering the ancient Greek civil war between Athens and Sparta, are master classes of character, virtue, justice, and human nature.

In contrast, Tom Holland is a contemporary of ours who specializes in secondary source history—meaning he more writes *about* history and primary sources. Among his works is the award-winning *Rubicon: The Triumph and the Tragedy of the Roman Republic*. Holland's precision and analysis are both coherent; better yet, they are contagious and will rub off on you.

Church history as a genre is on life support because today's church loves to feel superior to its past. The ecclesiastical historian Philip Schaff said, "The Church, not less than every one of its members, has its periods of infancy, youth, manhood, and old age."[6]

---

6. Philip Schaf, *The Principle of Protestantism as Related to the Present State of the Church* (Chambersburg, PA: Publication Office of the German Reformed Church, 1845), 51.

And how can one function in church life without a grasp of the church's previous epochs of growth? For sustained reading on the history of the church, one cannot do without Augustine, Eusebius, G. K. Chesterton, and Christopher Dawson. The first two are predominantly primary sources of church history (and ancients); the latter two are secondary sources (and modern). Caution: reading these four horsemen will make you incomparably aware of the exhilarating story of the church, in all her glory, and easily equip you to face today's unique challenges of the church, which shockingly look like the challenges faced by the ancient and medieval church.

In closing, a radical recovering of history is nonnegotiable for a robust Christianity. Let history be our North Star of delight. Herein looms the question, "How can we accomplish this and seize activation?" By adhering to the formula below:

History + Conviction + Compassion = Recovering of Robust Christianity

May we all recover the couplet of *conviction* and *compassion*—or certitude and affection, if you will—for history. These twin horses will pull history back strongly into the Circus Maximus of the Christian race, a race forged by the ancients. If our faith, *"that was once for all entrusted to God's holy people"* (Jude 1:3 NIV), has been waning in the West since the mid-twentieth century—societally and individually—it can emphatically be traced to our indifference of history and church history. But that will not be said of us on our watch.

> *Even to old age and gray hairs, O God, do not forsake me, until I proclaim your might to another generation, your power to all those to come.* (Psalm 71:18)

A caveat for social-justice-minded Christians: do not view history as a grievance study or a cloak for empty activism. Don't look for ammunition for your pet theological guns. Instead, view the ancient discipline as one to bring you awareness, complement your expanding intellect, and fill you with humility. You will find that resurrecting history will help to resuscitate the faith.

The world today looks in vain toward anyone who can lead the way with valiancy and virtue. Christian reader, *you* can be that leader. One who would wield the sword of history rightly, fairly, and prudently can never be lumped in with so many orphaned Christians of history who live today. Do not be like the wayward friends of Job about whom the Lord asked, *"Who is this that darkens counsel by words without knowledge?"* (Job 38:2).

With conviction steadily at your side and compassion's gleam in your eye, with possession of the past as your confident stride, may you be one of the few and the proud who helps to recover our Christian faith from its asthma-riddled race by exploring the eternal horizons of history.

12

RECOVERING OUR YOUTH

AUSTIN MOLT

Brace yourself for this tough pill to swallow: Gen Z is deconstructing their faith and changing their pronouns, all while giving away their personal information to China via TikTok. We are doomed.

Okay, calm down. I'm kidding. But what is not a joke is the rate at which young people are leaving the church. Increasingly, they are ditching the church and identifying as *spiritual but not religious*. Whether you are a young person, a parent, a youth ministry worker, a lead pastor, or just simply a Christian, you should care deeply about this issue because the future of the church will one day be in their hands.

MOVING BEYOND THE ALTAR

Growing up, I would go to the dentist's office against my will every six months for a routine cleaning. At one point, they would begin to dig into my gums with the floss. When they finished flossing and I had blood in my mouth and swollen gums, they would always ask the same dreaded question: "Austin, how often are you flossing at home?" I think it was evident to them that I lacked consistency in this area. Every time, I replied with, "I do sometimes, but I probably could be better about it." But no matter how good of a job they did flossing for me at my routine dental appointment, it wasn't going to fix my neglecting to floss at home.

As a youth pastor, I've often felt the way my dentist must have when I was growing up. There have been so many times over the past dozen or so years of youth ministry when a parent has called me to say, "My son is doubting if God is even real! Pastor, please meet with him and fix this!" But an hour-long conversation at a coffee shop discussing low-level apologetics isn't the solution for this kid who's on the brink of becoming an agnostic.

In the church I grew up in, I remember most of the encounters I had with God were at the altar. The altar was the area at the front of the stage, and my encounters would often take place at the end of the sermon, when there was some sort of call to action for someone to respond and go forward, usually accompanied by someone praying over you. I vividly remember responding to a lot of altar calls and walking forward. Some of those moments had a profound impact on my life. Evangelicals put an emphasis on having what we would call *an encounter with Jesus*. That Jesus is not simply an ideology that we adopt, but a person we can experience. This is true, but too often it seems to be out of balance. I've heard church leaders say, "An encounter with God changes everything!" These moments where we uniquely experience the presence of God can certainly be powerful, but there is a deeper question I've wrestled with for years now. I ask myself, "Are young people leaving the church because they need another encounter with God at the altar, or is there potentially something else we are missing?"

Imagine there is a married couple you know well who have been together for ten years but they're on the brink of divorce. They ask you for advice on what to do to get their marriage to a healthy place. I seriously doubt your advice would be that they just need to go have the best date night ever and that should do the job. Eat great food at a fancy restaurant, buy each other a sentimental gift, drink a glass of expensive wine, and then end the night with amazing sex. That isn't going to repair their marriage.

Do married couples need to prioritize one another and continue dating, pursuing one another, and working on their sexual intimacy? Of course they do. But one date night will not fix their lack of trust and the underlying issues that have been brewing for a long period of time. A *fresh encounter* in their marriage won't fix a deeply rooted problem. Have as many wonderful date nights as you want with your spouse. It still won't fix your marriage if you can't address past mistakes and work together moving forward with a new approach.

In the same way, an encounter with Jesus can be a catalyst moment in the life of a young person, but surely it is not the be-all and end-all.

There are many examples in the New Testament of people experiencing miraculous power during Jesus's ministry. At one point, Jesus healed ten lepers but only one returned to thank Him. (See Luke 17:11–19.) Students can be miraculously healed or have an experience with God at an altar call and still not follow Him. The Christian life is experiential, but it is also intellectual. *Repentance* in the New Testament means a change of mind.[1] For someone to follow Jesus, they must think differently.

Good marriages have wonderful experiences, but they aren't built on wonderful experiences. When I got married, I had to think differently because my entire life was now shared with someone else. A married man who thinks like a single man is on a fast track to the worst marriage ever. A young person in our church whose Christianity is built on experience is also in danger. Though they emotionally feel differently toward God, they still think like an unbeliever. In addition to our minds being transformed, our desires must be transformed as well. For example, I know that working out five days a week would be good for my health. The truth may be in my head, but it is not in my will.

Youth ministries today are putting on incredible events that fill arenas all over the USA. There are more resources online than we can count. Churches have embraced social media and have created online services for those who can't be there in person. Most churches have a paid youth pastor or, at minimum, volunteers who put on some sort of weekly program for young people. And yet young people are still leaving the church at an accelerated rate. Forty-one percent of Gen Z who confess to being Christians believe that church attendance is not important because it is

---

1. David Noel Freedman et al., *The Anchor Bible Dictionary* (New York: Doubleday, 1992), vol. 5, 672.

not relevant to their life.² With young people leaving the church in droves, at what point do we look at the data and think that we might need to take a different approach? We desperately need to think through how we lead young people beyond the altar.

LOOKING BACK TO MOVE FORWARD

Let's now look at how Martin Luther addressed a similar crisis in his day. As the Protestant Reformation began to gain momentum, it became obvious that there needed to be some sort of supervision over the churches. When Luther visited different congregations, he increasingly became more upset with the laity and those in leadership due to their laziness and lack of understanding of the Bible. He knew that coming out of the Roman Catholic Church, there needed to be an intentional way to create an identity for young people and new converts within the church. Luther decided to create what is called the small catechism and the large catechism. The word *catechism* means to orally instruct. Luther defined it this way, "Catechism is a form of instruction in which persons are questioned and asked to recite just as a schoolteacher has her pupils recite their lessons to determine whether they know them."

While the small catechism was written for children or someone new to the faith, the large catechism was written to train instructors. Luther envisioned the large catechism would be used to train three groups: pastors, public educators, and parents. As time went on, fewer and fewer parents were being trained; they were delegating their responsibility to catechize their children over to the leaders in the church. As Rev. Eric Jonas Swensson notes, "We see that in short order parents expected their children to be taught the Small Catechism by pastors and in school. Fathers were replaced by school teachers in the earliest years and then pastors when the children became youth."³

The idea of a catechism was not a new concept, but Luther's vision for it was unique. Where most catechisms were used to help the student

---

2. Barna Group, *Gen Z: The Culture, Beliefs and Motivations Shaping the Next Generation: A Barna Report Produced in Partnership with Impact 360 Institute*, vol. 1 (USA: Barna Group, 2018), 70.
3. Eric Jonas Swensson, "Luther's Catechism: How It Came to Be; What It Is; and How It Has Been Used," December 11, 2017; www.academia.edu/35405414.

memorize the content, he wrote his to help the student understand and apply it.[4] He put the Ten Commandments first so that one could recognize what God requires of them and how it is impossible for anyone to live up to His standards. Second, he included the Apostles' Creed so that we may see how we are rescued from our sin by the Triune God. Then, he adds in the Lord's Prayer so that we learn and practice how we can live the Christian life now that we are redeemed. Finally, he included the sacraments of the Eucharist and baptism so that we can understand how God meets us in our battle with the flesh.[5]

When I was growing up, I attended different events with guest speakers who shared their testimonies. Typically, their stories were relatively dramatic. I would hear about their life as a drug dealer, or how they spent time in prison, or how they were involved in a gang since the age of thirteen. Then, there was some crazy 180-degree turn in their life when they hit rock bottom, but it resulted in them giving their life to Jesus. The special speaker would end by saying, "I'm going to count to three. If you don't know that you know that you know you are going to heaven when you die and you want to be born again…on the count of three, I want you to lift your hand and pray this prayer with me!"

But my story is different. I loved going to church as a young person. Don't get me wrong, I have sinned a million times over, but I don't have some dramatic story that would go viral if posted on social media.

However, I've been in church long enough to know what the formula is: build a relationship with someone, invite them to church to hear the gospel, and then make sure they get discipled. Discipleship is the essential next step after someone makes a confession of faith, but that's not how it happened to me. I was discipled before I made a confession of faith.

It wasn't like my parents treated me like an agnostic until I turned thirteen years old. Imagine if they just decided they didn't want to indoctrinate me while I was growing up, so they avoided praying around me, didn't make me go to church with them, and shoved their Bibles away in their

---

4. Benjamin J. Tomczak, "Luther's Large Catechism: Its Historical Setting and Continuing Significance," presented at the Pastor-Teacher-Delegate Conference, South Central District of the Wisconsin Evangelical Lutheran Synod, January 22-23, 2009, 7; www.academia.edu/5854619.
5. Ibid., 8.

nightstand when I entered their room. Then one day when I was thirteen, they sat down with me to talk about different religions, saying, "So, Austin, we are going to cover what Muslims, Jehovah's Witnesses, Buddhists, and secular humanists teach. Following that, we'll go over Christianity, which is what your mom and I believe, but we don't want to put any pressure on you. This is totally your call because we don't want to influence you in this process."

The whole idea is absurd.

We are all being shaped by someone or something as we grow up. My story is that I was discipled before I ever made a confession of faith. But maybe a more accurate way to describe what happened early on in my life is that I was discipled *into* making a confession of faith. Now, of course, there are young people in the church without Christian parents. That is why spiritual fathers and mothers are so needed. But the point remains that parents are vital in shaping their children.

In Joshua 24, the Israelites must decide if they are going to recommit themselves to exclusively worshipping Yahweh or not. Yahweh is a jealous God and does not tolerate any rivals; He wants complete loyalty and allegiance. Although Israel functions as a nation, the covenant was a matter for each household.[6] That's why Joshua says:

> *And if it is evil in your eyes to serve the* LORD, *choose this day whom you will serve, whether the gods your fathers served in the region beyond the River, or the gods of the Amorites in whose land you dwell. But as for me and my house, we will serve the* LORD. (Joshua 24:15)

Being in covenant with God was a family matter, and it's a family matter still today. If I told my parents in middle school that I was no longer going to church with them, they would have chuckled at me. They had the same attitude as Joshua: *"As for me and my house, we will serve the* LORD."

I love it when people ask me when I was born again. I have no clue. It feels like asking me on which exact day I hit puberty. My allegiance and loyalty to Jesus were being instilled in me, formed in me, and intentionally

---

6. Bruce K. Waltke, "Joshua." In *New Bible Commentary: 21st Century Edition*, edited by D. A. Carson et al. 4th ed. (Downers Grove, IL: InterVarsity Press, 1994), 259.

role-modeled to me starting from my adolescence. Becoming a Christian is an event and a process.

Being born is an event that happens in an instant; growing up is a lifelong journey. Joining a gym takes a matter of minutes; getting in shape is, unfortunately, a long and grueling process. In the same way, some are discipled after they repent and follow Jesus in their adult years, and some are like Timothy, inheriting the faith of their parents and fanning the gift of God on them into flame as they mature. As Paul tells his young coworker:

> I am reminded of your sincere faith, a faith that dwelt first in your grandmother Lois and your mother Eunice and now, I am sure, dwells in you as well. For this reason I remind you to fan into flame the gift of God, which is in you through the laying on of my hands.
> (2 Timothy 1:5–6)

This is why catechism is so important. Most churches have a post-baptism discipleship method, but we also need a pre-baptism discipleship method. As Tom Crites says in *Why They Stay*:

> While there are no guarantees regarding whether a child who grows up in the church will continue as an adult, the research clearly revealed that as important as church experience is to those surveyed, the influence of the parents was of the greatest importance and sometimes navigated teens around bad church experiences.[7]

Every single youth pastor wants to see young people go the distance, and that is one of my biggest passions in life. Luther believed that the success or failure of Christianity hinged on whether parents were pastoring their children. In his 1522 sermon "The Estate of Marriage," he said:

> Most certainly father and mother are apostles, bishops, and priests to their children, for it is they who make them acquainted with the gospel. In short, there is no greater or nobler authority on earth

---

7. Dr. Steve R. Parr and Dr. Tom Crites, *Why They Stay: Helping Parents and Church Leaders Make Investments That Keep Children and Teens Connected to the Church for a Lifetime* (Bloomington, IN: WestBow Press, 2015).

than that of parents over their children, for this authority is both spiritual and temporal.

Pastors were to teach parents and parents were to teach their children. Considering Martin Luther and his work, what are we to do in the twenty-first century to see a shift take place among young people today? We desperately need to bring catechism back to our local churches. There are plenty of options available like *Luther's Small Catechism*, *Keach's Catechism*, *To Be a Christian: An Anglican Catechism*, and *The New City Catechism*. This will require the church to join forces with parents.

Churches and youth ministries are constantly trying to find ways to improve their programs, discipleship methods, and events. While we must continue to work at getting better in those areas, we need to recognize the benefit of catechism and the power it can have in building solid Christians from within the home. Raising children is not easy.

As a youth pastor, I don't want to just see a young person make a confession of faith and stop there. I want to see them become transformed from the inside out as a disciple of Jesus. Young people should encounter God. They need to learn Scripture in context. They need to be in church on Sundays and be pastored by those in spiritual authority. But in addition to all those essential and biblical things, young people need a home that teaches, demonstrates, and (dare I say) indoctrinates. The future of the church depends on it.

13

RECOVERING THE MINOR PROPHETS

LANDON MACDONALD

Do Marvel fans, on average, know more about their canon (collection of content) than Christians do about theirs? What about *Star Wars* fans? Or *The Office* aficionados?

Star Wars fans probably do, although I don't enjoy being a part of *Star Wars* fan culture because they fight more than first semester seminary reformed theologians.

Are there more Marvel fans who have watched all of the Marvel TV shows and movies than there are Christians who have carefully read the Minor Prophets?

If so, why?

I am not going for guilt here; I got enough of that at nine years of conservative Baptist Christian school. There are simply remarkable similarities in the comparison.

A marathon of *Star Wars* movies would take a hundred and thirty-one hours. The Marvel cinematic universe is about fifty hours long. *The Office* is ninety-nine hours long—a tad shorter than the ninety-hour Bible Reading Marathon at the U.S. Capitol every April as a prelude to the National Day of Prayer.[1]

Why is the general acceptance of fandom so low in Christianity? How long after someone becomes a fan of one of those series do they typically watch it all the way through?

Of all the content that gets overlooked in the Christian canon, the Minor Prophets are the most neglected.

Certainly, Leviticus has become some sort of meme to most people, a joke at a large church where the punch line is…what? That people don't enjoy the perfect Word of God proceeding from the Holy Spirit directly to our minds and lives?

I suppose the name doesn't help. "Minor Prophets" sounds kind of insulting. But Saint Augustine named them that to distinguish the twelve short prophetic books from the four longer books of the prophets Isaiah, Jeremiah, Ezekiel, and Daniel.

Regardless of their name, they are not minor in content, only in length. Be real though; this is the chapter you are most likely to skip. Right? Oh, man, I am getting saucy. Just know that while writing this, I am smiling, and I hope you are too.

The Minor Prophets should be of importance to us because they were of importance to God; He chose to inspire these prophets and include them in His book. Church fathers and people in church history got this, by the way. The New Testament includes thirty-two quotations or direct references to the Minor Prophets. The early church fathers also quoted them.

Which books of the Bible are read the most? Those containing the words of Christ, the Psalms, and Philippians 4 for its mental health advice. The least? Obadiah.[2]

Yes, Obadiah, the fourth minor prophet. He depicted the 1,200-year battle between Jacob's and Esau's descendants by two mountains, one in each territory. This is some *Lord of the Rings* type stuff, with *Game of*

---

1. See www.capitolbrm.org.
2. Jeffrey Kranz, "The least popular book of the Bible (it's not Leviticus)," May 9, 2014; overviewbible.com/least-popular-book-bible.

Thrones level pettiness. Millennial grudges are being carried out here. It's really cool stuff inside ancient Jewish prophetic poetry.

So why would that book be read the least of any? *It's the shortest book in the whole Old Testament!* I get it a bit though; Obadiah is the only minor prophet not quoted or referenced in the New Testament.

Or maybe there is some sort of weird subculture of people who have amalgamated Esau and his red hair into some sort of commentary on modern-day people with red hair. I have gotten some *wild* comments on a video I made about the book, seemingly because I have a red beard. (I am open to the idea of being called Red Beard, like some kind of pirate pastor.)

Why do people partially ignore this section of Scripture? Is it because the Minor Prophets are so complex and the most removed from the pleasure center of Scripture? Or is it perhaps because they encompass the parts of the Bible that most lend themselves to its poorest hermeneutic—that of the perpetual self-centered quiet time?

Whatever the case, these are the very words of God in these twelve ancient texts, and I would like to give you a few keys for recovering these incredible parts of Scripture with the space that I have left. I have probably made enough movie references already, right? I do not promise to stop though.

Okay, here are three elements that make the Minor Prophets specifically wonderful to teach and proclaim from, and why I believe you should not ignore but recover these parts of Scripture to reasonable and regular usage in your church, home, Bible study, meditation, and life.

1. THE MINOR PROPHETS POINT TOWARD CHRIST

You've got the classic wild ones like, *"Out of Egypt I called my son"* (Hosea 11:1), which I love because it is beautiful and true, but also because it breaks about 25 percent of the hermeneutical rules many are taught in Bible college. You've got the typological classics like Amos being a shepherd or the redemptive Shyamalan-esque *twist* ending at the end of the book, which of course could only come through the Messiah. You've got the classic clear prophecies like Micah about Bethlehem or Jonah in the whale for three days and three nights.

Any prophetic words of Christ are great wins as you study or teach because of the obvious ties to the largest narrative motif in Scripture—that of sin and redemption. These books add to that motif in their own way, as do the Books of Moses, the books of wisdom, and any section of Scripture. Having a fully formed theological view of any topic involves the complete gathering of items, stray or not, into a pile and looking at them all together. Many viewpoints in Scripture find their closest adherents in their local text neighbors.

Or to say it in another way, if millions of people cared about Jesus's face appearing on a pancake, then shouldn't this…I can't even finish it, it's so cheesy, but man, is it true. If you don't get the reference, then just Google it. Oh, you're conservative? Qwant it then. :)

2. THE MINOR PROPHETS SHOW THE TRAJECTORY OF GOD'S COVENANT WITH MOSES AND ISRAEL

God saw fit to show the full weight of many of His covenants through the Minor Prophets:

- The covenant with Abraham for a land; many were written in exile.
- The covenant with Abraham for a people; the Minor Prophets cast the future of this in appropriate doubt—not in relation to God keeping His promises, but in a sense providing many hints at the future grafting onto the existing tree.
- The covenant with Moses for blessing and cursing—I mean, let's be real, cursing is on full display here. The promise of blessings for obedience and curses for disobedience is the functional point of the book of Deuteronomy and a theme across the remainder of the Old Testament. Joshua obeys and is blessed; in Judges, the people disobey and are under a clear curse. Ruth obeys and is blessed; Solomon does both and gets both at various times. The Minor Prophets are written mostly at a time of exile, and the people of

Israel are clearly in a state of disobedience that has led to a direct curse that was specifically promised, being taken out of the land they were given.

- The covenant with David for a king; the waiting is clear, and the King is coming. Malachi is certainly clear on that.

The Minor Prophets continue these disparate but overlapping narrative threads that continue from when they begin to the book of Revelation.

As we learn and teach the Bible, it is these points, these moments, that serve as grapple holds for people looking to reach the summit. Like points of safety, refuge, or compass points,[3] they help us know where we are at and what is going on. As these covenants and promises move through these books and into the New Testament, we see clearly that although God chooses to change how He works sometimes, He Himself does not change, and His promises persist.

3. THE MINOR PROPHETS PROVIDE EXCRUCIATINGLY INTERESTING DETAILS

Here are twenty-six *wild* things that happen in the books of the Minor Prophets:

1. An army of darkness attacks a nation in a vision.
2. Israel is accused directly of worshipping a star god named Kiyyun.
3. People are accused of lying on an ivory bed, which sounds extremely uncomfortable…unless you had some sort of mattress situation.
4. Two prophets get into a verbal altercation that includes death threats (prophesies).
5. A famine of hearing God's words is threatened.
6. There's a vision of a basket of fruit.
7. There's a twist ending where the whole book is negative, but the end is incredibly positive.

---

3. Donald J. Wiseman, "General Preface," in *Obadiah, Jonah and Micah: An Introduction and Commentary*, vol. 26, Tyndale Old Testament Commentaries (Downers Grove, IL: InterVarsity Press, 1988), 7.

8. A prophet gets salty when his message is effective.
9. A man is eaten temporarily by a whale.
10. A man goes to Spain instead of where God asked him to go.
11. Dead bodies roll down a hill and turn to skeletons as they go.
12. Prophets are accused of only giving good prophecies when they get food from people as a gift.
13. People are prophesied to turn their swords into plows, exchanging war for farming in a time of peace.
14. A man attempts to grab a star in his hand as a metaphor.
15. The actual city Jesus will be born in is prophesied, and it is one of the smallest, most boring cities in the whole country.
16. An entire nation turns to God in one book, and they completely turn away a few generations later in a different book.
17. An evacuation in 1840 proves the accuracy of a prophesy issued 2,400 years earlier.
18. A book is addressed to the choir master like a psalm.
19. A book ends with a question.
20. God discusses the idea of basically redoing the flood.
21. God promises to make a man like a stunning piece of jewelry.
22. One prophet alone is quoted five times by Jesus Christ.
23. One prophesies of Jesus's return to the Mount of Olives; this time, it will split in two.
24. One prophet sees a vision of a red horse, and it's as terrifying as a Jordan Peele film.
25. One prophet sees eight visions.
26. One prophesies the return of Elijah.

A couple of those I made up. Want to find out which ones? Read the Minor Prophets.

In fact, let's recover the absolute *bonkers* nature of prophecy together because regardless of how wild and crazy it is, it's God's perfect Word, and we are its recipients.

If we show people the beauty hidden within mad visions and the gospel hidden in Micah and Pentecost hidden in Joel and more and more and more, we are doing something that has eternal value—showing people that *all* of God's Word is valuable, not just the parts that are easy for a quiet time.

We are in no danger of losing any parts of the Scripture. *"The grass withers, the flower fades, but the word of our God will stand forever"* (Isaiah 40:8). But each generation is in danger of missing out on or losing an excitement for the things that matter. That's on us. Let's recover that together—like the Bible says, teaching *"**the whole counsel** of God"* (Acts 20:27).

Okay, I have a few words left in the maximum word count I was given, so here is some more stuff that may help.

EACH MINOR PROPHET IN A PHRASE

Hosea: Israel and God's mercy

Joel: Israel and God's judgment

Amos: Israel and God's rebuke

Obadiah: Israel and God's enemies

Jonah: Israel and God's grace

Micah: Israel and God's uniqueness

Nahum: Israel and God's anger

Habakkuk: Israel and God's presence

Zephaniah: Israel and God's redemption

Haggai: Israel and God's house

Zechariah: Israel and God's visions

Malachi: Israel and God's money

Also, for whatever it's worth, I *do* like *Star Wars*, but fandom in popular art reaches a point of diminishing returns, while fandom in Scripture, if it leads to what Scripture teaches, should lead to belief, fruit, and obedience. God's Word has no diminishment at any point in life.

Oh, and Obadiah. I almost forgot. Not actually, though; this *is* a published book.

So more on Obadiah, the least-read book in the Bible. I call it a doom poem. Jerome says the book is difficult inversely proportionate to its small size.[4] And he allegedly despised his own commentary on the difficult book so much that he later burned it.[5]

A LITTLE BACKGROUND ON OBADIAH

The descendants of Abraham's grandson Jacob became Israel, while the descendants of Jacob's twin brother Esau became Edom. The brothers were *bitter* enemies, although they briefly reconciled on a surface level, and their respective nations were no different.

They warred for most of the Old Testament. You can read all about it in Numbers 20, 1 Samuel 14, 2 Samuel 8, 1 Kings 15, and 1 Chronicles 18.

Edom acted with evil and violence toward Israel, and it is great to see God being the loving protective Father here. He is *on* Israel for their sins and covenant unfaithfulness, but when someone threatens them, He steps in.[6]

In Obadiah 1:2, God says to Edom, *"Behold, I will make you small among the nations; you shall be utterly despised."* In verse 10, God says, *"Because of the violence done to your brother Jacob, shame shall cover you, and you shall be cut off forever."*

And to close the book, Obadiah 1:21 proclaims, *"Saviors shall go up to Mount Zion to rule Mount Esau, and the kingdom shall be the Lord's."* The mountains are both symbolic of the size and scope of this conflict and non-symbolic because there are actual literal mountains that their key

---

4. Leslie C. Allen, *The Books of Joel, Obadiah, Jonah, and Micah*, New International Commentary on the Old Testament (Grand Rapids, MI: William B. Eerdmans Publishing Co., 1976).
5. www.fourthcentury.com/jerome-first-commentary-on-obadiah.
6. Donald J. Wiseman et al., *Obadiah, Jonah and Micah: An Introduction and Commentary*, vol. 26, Tyndale Old Testament Commentaries (Downers Grove, IL: InterVarsity Press, 1988), 26.

cities are built on: Jerusalem for Mount Zion and Bozrah for Mount Esau. Charles H. Spurgeon confirmed this in his incredible, fifty-minute sermon just on verse 17.[7]

It's super simple! God judges the sinful, and God protects His covenant people. And it's also incredibly layered and rewards repeated reading and study. John H. Sailhamer points out there is a Balaam prophecy fulfilled here that I had not noticed.[8] It also has a clear salvific finale.[9]

Sorry, Jacob's brother! You lose! God wins. Which, of course, really happened.[10]

I suppose my point is this: if you had a safe full of love letters from your wife (which I do), would you read all of them? Yes, you would. So then, if we don't study or read a specific portion of the Bible, what does that mean about our belief in what the book claims about itself…or even more significantly, what are we missing that God's Spirit wrote for us?

You might be thinking, "Are you saying you wrote a whole chapter in a book that is basically saying to not skip these books?"

Yes! That was the point! Thank you!

---

7. Charles Haddon Spurgeon, "Possessing Possessions," sermon on Obadiah 17 from the Metropolitan Tabernacle Pulpit on March 23, 1890; www.spurgeon.org/resource-library/sermons/possessing-possessions/#flipbook.
8. John H. Sailhamer, "Obadiah" in *NIV Compact Bible Commentary* (Grand Rapids, MI: Zondervan, 1999).
9. J. Sidlow Baxter, *Baxter's Explore the Book: A Survey and Study of Each Book from Genesis Through Revelation* (Grand Rapids, MI: Zondervan, 1960), 137.
10. Ibid., 141.

14

RECOVERING CREATION

MATT VANNORSTRAN

People often ask me, "Are you a young-earth or an old-earth creationist?" To which I reply, "Neither. I am an *'In the beginning'* creationist." I endeavor to place priority upon the biblical text as set within its own context to produce a theology at home with Genesis's ancient audience as much as it should be with us. In his *The Lost World of Genesis One*, John H. Walton provides us with a possible approach to contextualizing the facets and aspirations of these early Genesis chapters, especially focusing upon the creation account's functionality to evidence climactic divine rest within the world as God's cosmic temple.[1]

In my developing stages as a young Christian, I often balked in ridicule at the outlandish "theories" of a big bang fourteen million years ago and evolutionary development. Why would I or anyone else need to look further than the opening pages of God's Word? For it is there stated that God created the material cosmos in six days approximately six thousand years ago, depending on how you structure your genealogical timelines.

---

1. John H. Walton, *The Lost World of Genesis One: Ancient Cosmology and the Origins Debate* (Downers Grove, IL: IVP Academic, 2009), 10–13.

Of course, I also conceived of this creation as a sphere revolving around the sun of a tiny system within the Milky Way as one of numberless galaxies in a wider universe, though none of this twenty-first-century information had been supplied to me by the King James Authorized Version of 1611.

One might assume exposure to a healthy dose of materials from fundamentalist yet scientific Christian groups would solidify the truth about origins I was so intentional about upholding. Such would need to be from a biblical standpoint primarily, of course, though only from sources of *non-atheistic* science.

After sorting through blurbs of information from groups like the Institute for Creation Research and even a few visits to the Creation Museum operated by Answers in Genesis, I couldn't help but slowly recognize some glaring inconsistencies. (Despite the many qualms I retain with the methodologies involved and stringently exclusivist conclusions, I would still recommend visiting the museum and the Ark Encounter, both located in Northern Kentucky.[2])

The fallibility of science was taken for granted, even expected, when it came to carbon dating. But these were Christians employing those very same scientific claims to support what they believed the first chapters of Genesis to say. Or rather, their interpretation of what they thought it to *mean*.

On one hand, I was expected to assume that the fossil layers could be proven as relatively recent in age, something to be arrived at through a complex system of geological hoops so that the earth appeared young.

On the other hand, and in the same breath, I was being told that the age of stars only appeared very old through their brightness and resultant temperature, therefore the light must have been instantaneously brought into the earth's view.

So why couldn't we reject the apparent age of starlight to agree with the supposedly incorrect carbon dating of fossils? Or how about we just explain the layers of sedimentary rock to only appear very old as if they were created that way?

---

2. creationmuseum.org; arkencounter.com.

For a time, the old-earth creationism of other believing science organizations such as Reasons to Believe was my place of solace. That way, I could still cling to the infallibility of my modernly literalistic approach to Genesis and simultaneously accept that *some* secular discoveries were shown as empirically supported.[3]

Yet I was absolutely against going the extra light-year, let alone a mile, to bridge the gap with those who held evolution and creationism as a possible combination like BioLogos for instance.

Nowadays, I'm not as certain—not due to a lack of information, clarification, or confidence, but more so because my assumptions and hubris have been tempered with time and experience.

Allow me here to clarify. I am not intending to lay out a particular case for an explicitly scientific approach to the mechanics of the universe. I am not a scientist, so it would be rash of me to offer any true appraisal of astrophysical, geomorphological, or evolutionary biological claims. But what I *can* do is read the Bible and proclaim with all my heart, mind, and strength that, *"In the beginning, God created the heavens and the earth"* (Genesis 1:1), regardless of what else that may entail.

Hermeneutics, the interpretation of scriptural texts, is an art.[4] It considers a variety of factors involving and interacting with the constituent parts of the Bible. Just as we do not read an editorial the same way we would read a historical novel, so also there are different ways to approach how we read the texts of Scripture.

Most people would advocate their own reading as the *plain, literal sense*—whether they are reading biblical poetry, prophecy, or parable. My response would concern the extent to which a person is handling the matters of original language and grammar, structure, literary features, historical context, intertextuality, canonical implications…the list of factors could go on.

---

3. This seems to be a consensus of popular conservative evangelical apologetics such as found in Lee Strobel, *The Case for a Creator* (Grand Rapids, MI: Zondervan, 2004).
4. Lee Roy Martin, *Biblical Hermeneutics: Essential Keys for Interpreting the Bible* (Miami, FL: Gospel Press, 2011), 11–19. This book can be used as a beginner's introduction to the arena of serious biblical interpretation.

We must then ask if an interpreter is imposing aspects of their own worldview onto and into the text. The paradigmatic lens through which we view the Bible determines a great deal regarding what we assume the text is saying. In trying to pull something out from the text, special care must be taken to not supply a meaning probably foreign to the author and intended audience.

The contents of Genesis, especially the first chapter, arose within a world vastly different from our own modern Western framework.

It was a domain of precarious yet bountiful life. The elements could be what afforded comfort or death. The mountains were treacherous to climb, and the seas were unexplored and untamable. The cycles of day and night, the weather, and seasons were as hoped for as the trees to give forth fruit and as feared as the ferocity of wild beasts. There was no science in the way we think of it in the present day. In that world, the natural order was indistinguishable from the supernatural.

Everything was explained as directly dictated by deities often at odds with one another, whose whims controlled the courses of history and personal destinies.

It was in this world that the Genesis account was breathed by God's Spirit to the mind of an ancient author for the sake of an ancient audience who saw the ancient world in ancient ways.

Would a Hebrew worshipper of YHWH from the bronze age really have thought about the narrative of creation freshly chiseled upon stone tablets in the way you do as a Christian in the digital age, accessing Genesis 1 on your electronic tablet?

At this point you might be asking yourself, "How, exactly, are we supposed to be transcribed into the position of someone from four millennia in the past?" First, we must become oriented within the biblical text since that is what we are primarily addressing.

But the key is to not bring a set of standards and questions pertaining to our current knowledge of cosmology and the way in which the world is known to us to work today. Instead, we want to step into the text and let it imaginatively build that immemorial realm around us to seek out the answers that the material is presenting.[5]

Questions that may arise out of the text might include thoughts such as, "Would Moses have used Genesis 1:1 as an introductory summary for what follows through the rest of the chapter? Or is it rather describing the initial step in the creative process of God?" If the former, then the functionality of what is brought together throughout the passage could be the focus of importance. If the latter, then it may be easier to conceive of an ancient portrayal for what theologians refer to as *creation from the new* or *creation out of nothing*. The Latin phrases are *creatio de novo* and *creatio ex nihilo*, respectively.[6]

Surprisingly, this concept can quickly take a turn into the philosophical, out of the text itself into various theories about the nature of material existence and God's relation to it.

That is a prime example of how easy it is for interpreters to turn aside on a trail leading away from the biblical content, while dragging the text along behind them. It devolves into a matter of seeking the right answers by using and abusing the wrong material.

In the case of those seeking to read modern scientific discoveries into the text, there is the issue of using one tool to redundantly do the job of another. If I wish to tighten a bolt, I do not reach for a hammer to pummel the object. Thus, as we seek to do theology, we should reach for the wrench of God's Word. When we want to nail down the science, we use a hammer.

The biblical text says the earth was desolately empty—in Hebrew, *tohu vabohu*, a curious phrase nominally associated with an empty wasteland in the prophetic writings. Isaiah 34.11 and Jeremiah 4.23 are the only places in the Hebrew canon where the words occur within close proximity to one another. Genesis 1:2 says there was only a watery depth covered in darkness. So did the ancient reader/hearer imagine the scene in the same way you or I naturally would? Thinking of a sphere suspended in an infinite

---

5. Walter Brueggemann, *Genesis: Interpretation: A Bible Commentary for Teaching and Preaching* (Atlanta, GA: John Knox Press, 1982), 13–14. Brueggemann's suggestion that imagination is where inspiration and creativity touch is a conscious stream throughout his work.
6. Donald K. McKim, *The Westminster Dictionary of Theological Terms*, 2nd ed. (Louisville, KY: Westminster John Knox Press, 2011), 73.

expanse of space? Would the audience be discussing how many millions of years might have passed between the first and second lines?

I highly doubt they would fret over how gravity must have functioned since a ball of solar energy 1.3 million times the size of the earth and a reflective moon rock fifty times smaller than Earth were not placed till three days later. Nor should we feel compelled to worry over these matters while progressing through this inspired narrative. Because the inerrancy of Genesis (and the rest of Scripture) resolutely lies here: there are no errors in the purposes and intentions with which the text was inspired, recorded, and preserved.

The differences existing between the description of God's creative work in Genesis and our present understanding of the material universe *in no way* impinge upon the truthfulness of Scripture. It does, however, make our *usage* of Scripture untruthful when we bend and contort it to fit the framework neither the human nor the divine author intended.

So, as we read of God's spoken word causing a separation between the primordial waters, we need not attempt a convoluted explanation for how this is *actually* an establishment of the atmosphere, portraying the waters above the separation as condensation, clouds, or whatever else we wish to conceptualize.

The Hebrew word for the resultant expanse in the midst of the water provides the idea of a solid firmament (a few points to the King James Version for getting it right), hardened like a metallic shield to suspend the waters above.[7]

And according to the text, the lights made on day four are only *"in the firmament"* (Genesis 1:14 KJV), not "above the firmament" as we know the sun, moon, and stars are exterior to the physical atmosphere.

This setup causes problems only for readers who expect the passage to scientifically detail the way we now understand the world to be. For the ancient Hebrews, however, it functioned as the perfect depiction of how they perceived God's creation to work. God was speaking to them in a way they could comprehend.

---

7. Francis Brown et al., *The Enhanced Brown-Driver-Briggs Hebrew and English Lexicon* (Oxford: Clarendon Press, 1977), 956.

God speaks to us through the same material, and it is entirely understandable when we read Genesis as a narrative composition written according to the paradigm of ancient Israel. It offers us theological truths that transcend time, distance, and cultural barriers. The problematic incomprehension comes only when we use pseudo-evidence to make cheap theology disguised in science parading around as inspired Scripture.

Certain relics preserved through history and archaeological discovery are another aid we may use for accustoming ourselves to the worldview of Genesis's original audience.

These documents create windows into ancient Near Eastern culture, whereby casting more light upon the annals of history. Such writings certainly do not impinge upon the priority and uniqueness of the biblical text, contrary to the arguments of those critical scholars rooted in modernity who assume de facto that we must accept a linear prototyping.[8]

But it would be folly to ignore the shared influences that must have existed between the Hebrews of the biblical world and the civilizations surrounding them. The most well-known among these traditional Mesopotamian texts is the *Enuma Elish*—meaning "When on High"—the story of creation dating to 1200 BC Babylon.[9]

In this epic, the god Marduk rises to prominence among a pantheon of greater and lesser deities by slaying the primeval being Tiamat, who personifies a deep watery abyss. By separating its corpse, Marduk forms the heavens and the earth with all of their details, including the luminaries, weather, dry land with its landscape, and rivers. Finally, another of the gods is slain so that the deity's blood can be used for the forming of humans—mortal creatures who may provide for Marduk so that he can relax.

It's a gory story, right? But surely one can see the reflective themes throughout: a depth of darkness, the necessity of separation, formation of humanity in likeness of the divine, and rest.

---

8. E. A. Speiser, *Genesis: Introduction, Translation, and Notes*, The Anchor Bible, vol. 1 (New York: Doubleday, 1963), 10.
9. This text and others can be found in collections such as James B. Pritchard, ed., *The Ancient Near Eastern Texts Relating to the Old Testament*, 3rd ed. with Supplement (Princeton, NJ: Princeton University Press, 1969), 60.

Hopefully one is also able to see the obvious differences.

Throughout the lore of classical Mesopotamian thought, similar themes abound.[10] To name a few, there is the Akkadian Atrahasis Epic, the Ugaritic Cycles of Baal, the Sumerian Eridu Tablet, Hittite Kumarbi Songs, and various Egyptian inscriptions.

Most likely, the majority of people have never even heard of, let alone read, any of these. That is because these texts, among many others that still lay dormant in the sands of the Middle East, are the domain of dusty scholars with nothing better to do.

It is by no means a coincidence that the most popular creation story leaps off the front page of the best-selling book in human history. The *Enuma Elish* didn't make it. Genesis did.

In the Genesis account, there is only one God, Elohim. It is by the creative power of His sheer will that everything is brought into being. No slaying, just the gentle breath of His Spirit brooding over the waters. At the command of His Word, the light and luminaries appear, a dome is made to cover sea and dry land, the vegetation springs forth, and then creatures of every shape and size fill the paradise. By the wisdom of His counsel, male and female are made in God's own image so they may steward a very good world and partake in the joyful rest of Sabbath.

So how did we get from there to here with all of our modern debates over science and Scripture? Many in the fundamentalist camp would prefer to claim their approach to Genesis remains the same as the rest of the historical orthodox faith.[11] That's a bit of a stretch. It's probably more accurate to claim continuity with post-Enlightenment Protestantism.

It may be surprising to realize that neither Christians nor the Jews themselves have ever had a monolithic, consistent approach to handling the text. For starters, throughout the Scriptures, there are other depictions of God's creative work. Job 38–41, Psalms 74 and 104, and Proverbs 8

---

10. Richard J. Clifford, *Creation Accounts in the Ancient Near East and in the Bible*, vol. 26, Catholic Biblical Quarterly Monograph Series (Washington, DC: Catholic Biblical Association, 1994), 1–10.
11. Ken Ham, "Rejoinder," in J. B. Stump, ed., *Four Views on Creation, Evolution, and Intelligent Design*, Counterpoints Bible & Theology (Grand Rapids: Zondervan, 2017), 67.

include examples from biblical Wisdom Literature wherein the details and order vary.

Philo of Alexandria, a prominently influential Jewish philosopher alive during the life of Jesus, popularized the idea that everything was produced in a moment of creative power. For him, Genesis gives us an orderly account via a structure of the week to depict how that instantaneous work transpired.[12]

Continuing this line of thought, many early Christian figures such as Clement and Athanasius viewed creation as an instant event while others took up some form of figurative meaning in the use of days.[13] Origen, himself being prone to wild theoretical ideas, expressed his position by complaining of those who took an overly literal approach:

> What man of intelligence, I ask, will consider it a reasonable statement that the first and the second and the third day, in which there are said to be both morning and evening, existed without sun and moon and stars, while the first day was even without a heaven?[14]

Because of his immense impact upon later medieval theology, especially concerning creation, Augustine is particularly useful to this discussion. This fourth and fifth century AD saint not only wrote multiple commentaries on Genesis, but the idea of creation takes up a large portion of content in his more personal writings. Perhaps this is because he was converted to the Christian faith only after hearing the preaching of Ambrose from the creation text, who proclaimed its figurative nature instead of a literal one.[15]

Augustine's first commentary on Genesis addressed such allegorical readings, while his second commentative attempt was geared toward a literal reading. Yet, Augustine's definitional understanding for "literal" was

---

12. Philo, *On the Creation* 13–15, trans. F. H. Colson, G. H. Whitaker, and J. W. Earp, vol. 1, *The Loeb Classical Library* (Cambridge, MA: William Heinemann Ltd; Harvard University Press, 1929–1962), 13.
13. Andrew J. Brown, *The Days of Creation: A History of Christian Interpretation of Genesis 1:1–2:3*, History of Biblical Interpretation (Blandford Forum, UK: Deo, 2014), 26–31.
14. Origen, *On First Principles* 4.3.1, trans. G. W. Butterworth (New York: Harper & Row, 1966), 288–89.
15. Gavin Ortlund, *Retrieving Augustine's Doctrine of Creation: Ancient Wisdom for Current Controversy* (Downers Grove, IL: IVP Academic, 2020), 119.

that the symbolic language in the narrative does correspond to what happened, though he admits he does not definitively know how. At the end of this literal commentary, he concludes:

> I have discussed the text and written down as best I could in eleven books what seemed certain to me, and have affirmed and defended it; and about its many uncertainties I have inquired, hesitated, balanced different opinions, not to prescribe anyone what they should think about obscure points, but rather to show how we have been willing to be instructed whenever we have been in doubt as to the meaning, and to discourage the reader from the making of rash assertions where we have been unable to establish solid grounds for a definite decision.[16]

And in his *Confessions*, Augustine laments:

> For when I hear any Christian brother ignorant of these things, and mistaken on them, I can patiently behold such a man holding his opinion; nor do I see that any ignorance as to the position or character of the corporeal creation can injure him, so long as he doth not believe anything unworthy of Thee, O Lord, the Creator of all. But it doth injure him, if he imagines it to pertain to the form of the doctrine of piety and will yet affirm that too stiffly, whereof he is ignorant.[17]

I consider that much benefit would be wrought if current Christian discussion surrounding creation, the biblical text, and scientific discovery could take on the attitude of Augustine once again.

It would benefit our views of creation by affirming those theological truths most central to its intentions—namely God's power, purpose, and praise.

It would benefit our treatment of the text by letting Genesis speak for itself without reading modern stipulations into it.

---

16. Ibid., 68, "The Missing Virtue in Science-Faith Dialogue: Augustine on the Importance of Humility," per his translation of *De Genesi ad litteram* 12.1.1 (CSEL 28:1, 379).
17. Augustine Bishop of Hippo, *The Confessions* 5.5, trans. E. B. Pusey (Oak Harbor, WA: Logos Research Systems, Inc., 1996).

It would benefit our relationship with science by remembering that whatever discoveries are made, it's still about God's universe.

Whereas today's science can become tomorrow's myth, God's Word stands forever.

15

RECOVERING JUSTICE: DOING GOOD FOR GOD'S GLORY

CHRISTINA CRENSHAW

A couple of years ago, I led a workshop titled "How the Church Can Combat Human Trafficking" at a large annual Christian missions' conference in Oregon. Afterward, about half a dozen attendees lingered to ask follow-up questions. In retrospect, I couldn't tell you anything particularly unique about these attendees or their questions. They struck me as a common group of evangelicals with a heart for reaching the lost with the gospel. However, I did meet one young lady who I think about often and likely won't soon forget.

Unlike the other attendees, who were in their thirties and forties, well out of college and into their ministry or professional work, this young lady was still in college. Her age alone set her apart from the group, but mostly, I was taken aback by her follow-up question and the resolve she exuded when asking it. When the line dwindled and she reached me, she got straight to the point and with confidence beyond her years stated, "I feel called to do justice work. When I finish college, I want to do justice for Jesus. How can I find a job doing that?" What struck me most about her question wasn't just the astute theological juxtaposition of doing good work for kingdom purposes, which alone was impressive at her age. Rather, I was most surprised by the phrase *justice for Jesus*. Maybe it was the punch-packed alliteration, but I really liked the sound of that.

As it turns out, this young lady is not so unique for her age demographic. Generally speaking, Millennials and Gen Z generations have a strong inclination to engage social justice issues, and that is a genuinely admirable attribute. In my fifteen years of teaching college students, I have seen this passion for engaging good evidenced time and again in my classroom. And although doing social justice work isn't necessarily exclusive to those under the age of thirty, according to the latest research from Pew, Barna, and Lifeway, it is an indicative characteristic of those in the Millennial and Gen Z generations, arguably more so than other generations in living history.[1] It's apparent these generations value working toward the common good, which should be applauded and encouraged.

But as followers of Christ, our resolve for doing social justice is found in Jesus, rather than in hopes that our contribution will somehow yield a better, more just society. Our impetus for feeding the hungry, clothing the poor, caring for orphans and widows, and freeing those enslaved is not rooted in humanist, socialist frameworks for working toward the common good. There is certainly enough common grace to partner with those efforts. But if the Bible is our touchstone for truth and our motivation for loving others well, then our reasons for doing good unto our neighbors will be vastly different than someone engaging in similar efforts from a secular framework. Our work will be done in the spirit of gathering around a common theological understanding of justice not centered on a humanist, secular approach but rather rooted in a biblical framework and church orthodoxy.

In spite of what the contemporary cultural narrative may lead us to believe, social justice work is not actually an invention of postmodern ideology nor is it unique to progressive Christianity. In the Gospels and throughout the New Testament, we witness Jesus and His followers' concern for the spiritual and social welfare of all people, particularly the marginalized, disenfranchised, and victimized. Early church leaders

---

1. Barna Group, *The Connected Generation: How Christian Leaders Around the World Can Strengthen Faith & Well-Being Among 18-35-Year-Olds*, 2019.

understood the importance of orthodoxy and orthopraxy and integrated these values into church doctrines and creeds.

And throughout church history, faithful Christian leaders have been at the heart of dynamic communities working toward the common good from a biblical worldview. Third century leaders such as Saint Basil the Great, Saint John Chrysostom, and Saint Augustine of Hippo beseeched both Christians and Romans to care for the economic welfare of the people and care overall for the vulnerable.[2] In the early thirteenth century, Christians called for more accountability among nobility and freedoms for commoners in the Magna Carta, which was a revolutionary treaty for its time. Historians widely consider this treaty a significant inspiration for many of America's founding documents such as the Declaration of Independence, the United States Constitution and the Bill of Rights, the United Nations' Universal Declaration of Human Rights, and the British Human Rights Act.[3]

But where the authors of those documents failed to uphold Christian political ethics, others would later rise to the occasion. William Wilberforce and John Newton, for instance, were key religious leaders at the heart of the nineteenth century British abolition movement. And in America, key figures such as Frederick Douglass, W. E. B. DuBois, Sojourner Truth, Harriet Tubman, and Booker T. Washington would also reference Scripture as an impetus for ending slavery and honoring the *imago Dei* of every human.[4] In more contemporary times, we find examples of faith-informed justice work in the efforts of people like Rev. Martin Luther King Jr., Mother Teresa, and Chuck Colson, who reminded us to work toward racial reconciliation, mitigating poverty, and prison reform.

These historical Christian leaders, and many more like them, have worked for justice, mercy, and peace from a biblical understanding of these concepts. God's redemption and restoration are the pillars on which they have engaged culture; kingdom-minded purposes and cultural renewal have been at the heart of their efforts. Church history tells of their efforts to establish community centers, preventative health care and rehabilitation

---

2. John D. Hannah, *Invitation to Church History: World* (Grand Rapids, MI: Kregel Academic, 2018).
3. Ibid.
4. Ibid.

services, counseling facilities, schools, hospitals, libraries, orphanages, and so forth. Christian agents of change know that they are doing the work of Christ when they show compassion to *"the least of these"* (Matthew 25:40).

Faithful followers of Christ understand their vocational responsibility to be an agent of change within the context of the biblical narrative, but within the context of contemporary Western culture, Christians must also grapple with the role of the church in an increasingly post-Christian and pluralistic society. In what meaningful ways might Christians engage social issues and participate in social innovation in the public square? How do our efforts to engage justice differ from those of people who do not share our faith? And more specifically, how might we now mobilize the church to work for the common good?

WORLDVIEW: UNDERSTANDING OUR LENS FOR LIFE

Foremost, applying a biblical framework to justice requires we understand how our worldview influences every facet of our being. In brief, a worldview is a person's core set of beliefs and values, an integrated framework of learned and shared beliefs and behaviors that help give meaning to life, death, and the purpose for both. It is a framework for how to consider and engage life through this lens. It encompasses values, customs, principles, and actions—all of which bind a society together and establish a sense of identity, purpose, and solidarity within a community.

A person's worldview is profoundly important, as it determines how their life is lived. As you can imagine, the more cohesive the worldview of families, groups, organizations, and communities, the more commonality shared within the macro-cultural ethos. Someone with a distinctly Christian worldview has a Christlike mindset about life. A Christian worldview is derived from Scripture and provides answers to existential life questions such as, "Where did we come from? Who are we? What has gone wrong with the world? What solution can be offered to fix it?"

David Dockery, a prominent scholar, says this about the Christian worldview:

For Christians to respond to the world's challenges we must hear afresh the words of Jesus from what is called the Great Commandment (Matt. 22:36-40). Here we are told not only to love God wholeheartedly with our hearts and souls, but with our minds as well. Jesus' words refer to a wholehearted devotion to God with every aspect of our being, from whatever angle we choose to consider it—emotionally, volitionally, or cognitively.[5]

In short, applying a Christian worldview is to rightly see life through a biblical lens that by God, through God, and for God, all things were created; we have fallen, but can be redeemed and restored by Him. Everything is His, and anything outside the will of God is in need of redemption and restoration, just like mankind. On this, theologian Abraham Kuyper conveyed the Lord's dominion well when he stated, "There is not a square inch in the whole domain of our human existence over which Christ, who is Sovereign over all, does not cry, Mine!"[6] In other words, we trust our worldview to God because He is the creator of our world and sovereign over all.

VOCATION: UNDERSTANDING OUR PURPOSE AND CALLING

Just as our understanding of the Christian worldview matters for engaging justice work, so does our understanding of our vocational call to do so. And much like studying worldview, vocation also has historical, distinctly Christian roots. The term actually has a beautiful and multifaceted history that dates back to the early church. In contemporary times and in more secular spheres, vocation frequently refers to *work*, but the Latin definition, *voci*—to be called or summoned by the Creator—is a distinctly sacred notion. One of the most celebrated modern definitions of vocations comes from the late theologian Frederick Buechner who states, "The place

---

5. David S. Dockery, *Faith and Learning: A Handbook for Christian Higher Education* (Nashville, TN: B&H Publishing Group, 2012).
6. Abraham Kuyper, *Wisdom & Wonder: Common Grace in Science & Art* (Grand Rapids, MI: Christian's Library Press, 2011).

God calls you to is the place where your deep gladness and the world's deep hunger meet."[7]

This is certainly a good place to start, and it speaks quite well to our generational cry for justice. Buechner describes God as a caller, one who loves us enough to pursue our heart's desires. Buechner rightly places equal importance on the whole of humanity and our individuality. He juxtaposes our heart's desires with the world's great needs and then implies God cares profoundly about both. Buechner illuminates a divinely symbiotic relationship between the world and the use of our vocation, both created by the Caller to bring Him glory.

The very essence of calling is that God designed us for a specific purpose and endowed us with unique gifts. Several passages in Scripture indicate we are uniquely gifted and called by God. (See Romans 12:6–8; 1 Corinthians 12:8–10, 28–30; Ephesians 4:11.) The Lord calls us to serve Him in our spheres of influence in ways that affirm our predispositions, gifts, desires, and strengths but also meet the world's needs. He endows us with a calling so that our work may be done not only for the sake of our world but also for the sake of His kingdom purposes. This is a central teaching in a biblical understanding of vocation. A biblical worldview approach to our vocation gives purpose to the work we are called to do and to the gifts we've been given.

With this perspective, there is no distinction between the mission field and the professional world. In fact, all efforts done for the glory of God are considered holy in His kingdom economy. I like how A. W. Tozer phrases this notion in *The Pursuit of God* when he writes, "It's not what a man does that determines whether his work is sacred or secular; it is why he does it."[8] Our roles, our positions, and our employment may change, but our vocational ministry does not. God's call on our lives—to use what He has given us for His glory—remains. In and out of season, we are vocationally called to do good work, like justice, unto the Lord.

---

7. Frederick Buechner, *Wishful Thinking: A Theological ABC* (New York: Harper & Row, 1973).
8. A. W. Tozer, *The Pursuit of God: The Human Thirst for the Divine* (Chicago, IL: Moody, 2015).

STEWARDSHIP: UNDERSTANDING WHY WE DO JUSTICE

Perhaps one of the more impactful ways we integrate our Christian worldview and our vocational call is in the way we steward justice. We tend to think of stewardship in terms of financial management and generosity, and that's certainly an important aspect of it. But even more, stewardship embraces human flourishing, and that includes social justice for the welfare of others. How we see the world and engage our vocation is stewardship. This authentic integration speaks not only to how much we love God but also to how much we love others with His love.

Almost anyone can gather around biblical principles of justice like loving kindness and walking humbly (Micah 6:8), visiting *"orphans and widows in their affliction"* (James 1:27), and loving our neighbor (Matthew 22:39). Within this framework, there is a common grace for all of us to engage the common good. So, it's not uncommon for nonbelievers to engage social justice work, and the outcome of their efforts may look very similar to someone doing good work from a Christian worldview. What differentiates social justice from biblical justice is less in our methods or outcomes and more in our motives.

There are varying definitions of what constitutes justice, but I especially like how Timothy Keller distinguishes the differences of definitions and motives in his book *Generous Justice*. To paraphrase his thoughts, social justice is deconstructing traditional systems and structures thought to be oppressive and redistributing power, resources, and finances in ways that better ensure the equality of outcomes. Biblical justice, on the other hand, is conformity to God's moral standard, obedience to His commands, and the pursuit of what He deems right, just, and holy. In brief, social justice is common good work done unto society, but biblical justice engages broken, fallen places from a profound understanding of God's grace. And the work is done unto His glory, not merely for the improvement of society.

One of my favorite quotes in Keller's *Generous Justice* captures the essence of how God's grace moves us to justice:

For indeed, grace is the key to it all. It is not our lavish good deeds that procure salvation, but God's lavish love and mercy. We see that God cares about the poor, that his laws make provision for the disadvantaged. God's concern for justice permeated every part of Israel's life. It should also permeate our lives.[9]

If God is the author of justice, then apart from Him, all of our definitions, descriptions, and theoretical frameworks are insufficient. The Lord calls us to be just and love our neighbors; when that is our heart's motive, then the stewardship of our resources for the good of others becomes an expression of both our love for Him and His love for humanity.

PARTNERING WITH THE CHURCH

I've found there is no better place to do good work and love our neighbors than in the church body. The church won't engage justice perfectly because it is composed of imperfect people. But in two thousand years, the body of Christ has a much better track record of loving others well and meeting their needs better than the rest of the world does. If we want to do justice, we want to first consider whose version of justice we are enacting. We should ask ourselves by what standard, measurement, and purpose are we doing our good work? Are we doing it merely unto humanity for the sake of improving society, or are we serving fellow image-bearers of God for His glory so they may come to know Jesus?

Our worldview, our vocation, and our stewardship of all God has given us should lead us to compassion, justice, and mercy. So, church, let's do *justice for Jesus*—yes and amen. But may we first attune our hearts to His heart, partner with His bride, and engage good work according to the His definition of justice and not merely culture's. May the Lord be glorified by our work and may our efforts lead others to His gospel of redemption and restoration.

---

9. Timothy Keller, *Generous Justice: How God's Grace Makes Us Just* (New York: Penguin Publishing Group, 2012).

RECOMMENDED BIBLE VERSES AND BOOKS FOR FURTHER READING

WORLDVIEW

Matthew 4:17; Romans 12:2; 1 Peter 1:14; Colossians 2:20–23; 1 John 2:15–17

Philip Graham Ryken, *Christian Worldview: A Student's Guide* (Wheaton, IL: Crossway, 2013)

VOCATION

Colossians 3:12–17; Romans 8:28; 2 Corinthians 5:17–20; Genesis 2:15, 19–20

Gordon T. Smith, *Courage and Calling: Embracing Your God-Given Potential* (Downers Grove, IL: InterVarsity Press, 2011)

JUSTICE

Hebrews 10:24–25; 1 Corinthians 9:20–23; Amos 5:15; Hosea 12:6; James 1:27

Timothy Keller, *Generous Justice: How God's Grace Makes Us Just* (New York: Penguin Publishing Group, 2012)

16

RECOVERING OUR CARE FOR THE PERSECUTED

GIA CHACÓN

Christians are the most persecuted religious minority. Yes, you read that correctly. Although Christians constitute the largest religious group in the world, in many countries, Christians are a minority and face targeted hostility solely because of their faith.

Although persecution is nothing new to the body of Christ, you might be surprised to learn that there are more Christian martyrs today than at any other time in church history. In fact, over 360 million believers around the world face high levels of persecution.[1] Our brothers and sisters are facing imprisonment, torture, and even death because of their faith—and the crisis of Christian persecution has consistently *worsened* for the past five years.[2] Knowing this, we must ask ourselves why there is silence around this issue today, when taking care of the persecuted was a paramount concern for the faithful for centuries up until about sixty-five years ago. Why has the Western church forgotten its duty to the suffering faithful? We must recover our care for the persecuted.

---

1. "World Watch List 2023," www.opendoorsus.org/en-US/persecution/countries.
2. Ibid.

Chaldean Christians (Christians from Iraq) have suffered some of the most horrifying and tragic persecution in recent history. In one generation, Iraq's Christian population has decreased over 80 percent.[3] The Nineveh Plain, which was once a bastion of Christianity in the Middle East, is now a wasteland of bombed and desecrated first-century churches and mass graves of religious minorities. This destruction was done at the hands of radical Islamist groups, primarily ISIS (the Islamic State of Iraq and Syria), in a futile attempt to not only kill all Christians in the region, but also to erase the rich history of Christianity from the country altogether.

I recall a story told to me by Father Simon Essaki, a Chaldean Catholic priest in the eparchy of San Diego, California, and a close friend of mine. He visited Iraq a few years after ISIS had been militarily defeated and traveled with the regional bishops to the churches that had been destroyed. Simon told me he visited a church in Nineveh where terrorists stormed a Sunday service and massacred over forty worshippers, including two priests. He recounted entering the church and seeing the blood of the martyrs stained into the floor and left as a testimony of their ultimate sacrifice for Jesus Christ.

However, Christians aren't just suffering in Iraq. They are also suffering under the communist regimes of China and North Korea. They are facing unprecedented violence in Africa. In 2022 alone, over two thousand Christians were slaughtered in Nigeria.[4] In Nicaragua, the government is kidnapping and imprisoning priests and bishops who dare speak out against the authoritarian rule of President Daniel Ortega.[5] Christians face persecution in over fifty countries,[6] yet we hear almost nothing of their plight from the pulpits of the churches in the West.

So what should our response be to the suffering of our brothers and sisters around the world?

---

3. "Global Prayer Guide: Iraq," *The Voice of the Martyrs*; www.persecution.com/globalprayerguide/iraq.
4. "Jihadists Killed 2543 Nigerian Christians in 2022," *Intersociety International Report* (Vol.2: 2022); www.genocidewatch.com/single-post/jihadists-have-murdered-2543-nigerian-christians-in-2022.
5. "Nicaragua Silences Its Last Outspoken Critics: Catholic Priests," *New York Times*; www.nytimes.com/2022/08/23/world/americas/nicaragua-catholic-church-daniel-ortega.html.
6. Open Doors USA, "World Watch List 2023."

THE BEGINNING OF PERSECUTION

To answer this question, we must first examine what's commonly referred to as the "beginning of persecution" in Scripture. In Acts 4, we read the story of Peter and John, who were brought before the Sanhedrin, threatened, and ordered *"not to speak or teach at all in the name of Jesus"* (Acts 4:18). When Peter and John refused, they were released with more threats, and they immediately returned to the community of believers to tell them what had happened. The believers knew that persecution was going to follow, but instead of praying for protection from the persecution, they prayed for boldness. (See Acts 4:29.) Following this incident, the apostles faced pressure and violence for continuing to preach and teach in the name of Jesus, but we see a *shift* in the body of Christ as a result of the first intentional killing of a Christian.

Enter Stephen, the protomartyr—Christianity's first martyr. In Acts 7, we read the account of the stoning of Stephen for his testimony of Christ. What's to follow this event is our focus. As a result of Stephen's testimony and martyrdom, Scripture tells us, *"There arose on that day a great persecution against the church in Jerusalem, and they were all **scattered** throughout the regions of Judea and Samaria, except the apostles"* (Acts 8:1).

Tertullian wrote, *"Plures efficimur, quotiens metimur a vobis: semen est sanguis Christianorum,"*[7] which is commonly and liberally translated as, "The blood of the martyrs is the seed of the church." The more literal translation of Tertullian's words would be, "We multiply when you reap us. The blood of Christians is seed."

How is the blood of Christians *seed*? Perhaps when you read this quote, you envision a single, solitary seed being placed into the ground to produce a single plant. However, when a farmer is planting in his field, he *scatters* seeds to get as much across the field as possible, to grow as many plants as possible in order to reap the greatest harvest. When we look at the blood of Christians as *seed*, we should envision that as a result of persecution, the believers are scattered as seed across a field to produce a greater harvest—more believers.

---

7. *Apologeticus*, L. 13.

We see this in Acts 7 and 8. Following the martyrdom of Stephen and the persecution of believers that ensued, the believers were scattered and *thus the gospel was spread.*

Now those who were scattered went about preaching the word.

(Acts 8:4)

This concept is what I call *the paradox of persecution*. When the church is persecuted, rather than extinguishing the fervor of believers, it produces bold Christians who proclaim Christ, thus causing the gospel to spread.

We also learn in Scripture what our responsibility is toward those who are persecuted. Hebrews 13:3 says, *"Remember those who are in prison, as though in prison with them, and those who are mistreated, since you also are in the body."* Let's unpack this biblical mandate given to us by Saint Paul in his letter to the Hebrews.

If we read the original Greek translation of this verse, we will first notice that the word "remember" is the Greek word *mimnēskesthe*, which means to actively remember.[8] This translation means there is a "high level of *personal* (self) involvement and *personal* interest motivating this remembering."[9] By understanding the true definition of the word "remember" in this context, we can clearly recognize that the author's intention was to command believers to *actively call to mind* those who are imprisoned and mistreated. This was not a light suggestion, but rather a mandate of responsibility to *pray for* those who are imprisoned and persecuted.

Why? Paul makes it very clear that we are to pray for those imprisoned as if we were imprisoned also *because we are part of the body of Christ*. We know also from 1 Corinthians 12:26 that when one member of the body suffers, all suffer with it. So we understand that we are in no way separated from our brothers and sisters who are imprisoned and mistreated, but rather, we being part of the body of Christ have a *responsibility* to remember the persecuted with the same level of personal interest that we would have if we were imprisoned with them.

Again, this is not a light suggestion. In fact, for centuries, the church has taken this responsibility with the utmost seriousness and urgency.

---

8. 3403. mimnéskó. *Strong's Greek Concordance.*
9. Ibid.

A BRIEF HISTORY OF THE PERSECUTION OF THE CHURCH

The persecution of the church began in the era of the apostles and has continued ever since. First century Christians were persecuted by both the Jews and the Roman Empire. As we course through the New Testament, we read the accounts of the believers persecuted at the hands of the Jewish religious leaders or the Sanhedrin. Even Saint Paul—named Saul of Tarsus before his conversion on the road to Damascus—is introduced to us at the end of Acts 7 and the beginning of Acts 8 as approving the stoning of Stephen.

> *Then they cast him out of the city and stoned him. And the witnesses laid down their garments at the feet of a young man named Saul. And as they were stoning Stephen, he called out, "Lord Jesus, receive my spirit." And falling to his knees he cried out with a loud voice, "Lord, do not hold this sin against them." And when he had said this, he fell asleep.* ***And Saul approved of his execution.*** (Acts 7:58–8:1)

Under the Roman Empire, believers were first persecuted for their refusal to make sacrifices to false gods and idols. In the first century, Rome was a polytheistic society, and citizens regularly made both public and private sacrifices to their gods.[10] Christians who refused to make these sacrifices were often accused of treason, crimes, and involvement in cults that led to apostasy. One famous persecution of Christians began in AD 64, when Emperor Nero used the Christian community as a scapegoat for the uncontrollable fires that burned throughout Rome for six days.[11]

That era gave way to the martyrdom of incredible witnesses of the faith such as Saint Polycarp, bishop of the church in Smyrna (modern-day Izmir, Turkey). According to an account written of his martyrdom in the second century, around AD 160, Polycarp was arrested by Roman soldiers and taken to an arena, where they tried to convince him to deny Christ in order to save his life. The Roman proconsul said to Polycarp, "Reproach Christ and I will set you free!" To which Polycarp responded, "Eighty-six

---

10. William C. Morey, *Outlines of Roman History* (New York: American Book Company, 1901); www.forumromanum.org/history/morey03.html.
11. Stephen Dando-Collins, *The Great Fire of Rome: The Fall of the Emperor Nero and His City*, citing *The Annals of Tacitus* 15:44 (Boston, MA: Da Capo Press, 2010).

years have I have served him, and he has done me no wrong. How can I blaspheme my King and my Savior?"

Polycarp's punishment was to be burned alive. As the Romans prepared a fire for the saint, Polycarp prayed the following prayer:

> O Lord God Almighty, the Father of your beloved and blessed Son Jesus Christ, by whom we have received the knowledge of you, the God of angels, powers and every creature, and of all the righteous who live before you, I give you thanks that you count me worthy to be numbered among your martyrs, sharing the cup of Christ and the resurrection to eternal life, both of soul and body, through the immortality of the Holy Spirit. May I be received this day as an acceptable sacrifice, as you, the true God, have predestined, revealed to me, and now fulfilled. I praise you for all these things, I bless you and glorify you, along with the everlasting Jesus Christ, your beloved Son. To you, with him, through the Holy Ghost, be glory both now and forever. Amen.

The fire blazed, but miraculously Polycarp's body would not burn. Finally, the soldiers demanded an executioner stab him in the chest and Saint Polycarp died. His witness for Christ is celebrated to this day.[12]

The suffering that Christians endured under the Roman Empire continued until Constantine the Great published the Edict of Milan in AD 313, which gave legal status to Christianity and protected Christians from persecution.

The early Middle Ages saw the beginning of the persecution of Christians under Islam. According to one account, the Prophet Muhammad said, "I will expel the Jews and Christians from the Arabian Peninsula and will not leave any but Muslim."[13] As a result, Christians were treated as second-class citizens compared to Muslims and forced to pay a heavy *jizya* tax for being non-Muslim. Believers were also prohibited from constructing new churches, forced to wear humiliating clothing, and enslaved. Christians were banned from proselytizing and faced death if

---

12. *The Martyrdom of Polycarp*, translated by J. B. Lightfoot, abridged and modernized by Stephen Tomkins; christianhistoryinstitute.org/study/module/Polycarp.
13. Sahih Muslim 1767a, *The Book of Jihad and Expedition*.

caught doing so. These ideologies remain throughout the Middle East and much of the Muslim world to this day.

Beginning in the twentieth century, Christians faced persecution under communist and socialist regimes such as the Chinese Communist Party and the former Soviet Union. These regimes sought to eliminate organized religion; to achieve this goal, they destroyed churches, synagogues, and mosques and imprisoned religious leaders, along with anyone who refused to renounce their faith. It is reported that between 12 million and 20 million believers were killed before the collapse of the Soviet Union in 1991.[14] In China, millions were killed and thousands imprisoned during Mao Zedong's antireligious campaign. To this day, the Chinese Communist Party targets Christians by imprisoning pastors and church leaders, destroying and removing crosses from churches, and forcing believers into reeducation or concentration camps.[15] Such regimes seek to control their citizens and see religion, especially Christianity, as a threat to their power.

MARTYRS ARE WITNESSES

In today's understanding of the word, *martyr* means a person who is killed because of their beliefs, usually religious. However, the original Greek word μάρτυς or *martus* is defined as "a witness."[16] In biblical context, a martyr is someone who *bears witness* to the testimony of Christ. Over time, the word evolved to mean someone who dies for their religious beliefs because bearing witness to the testimony of Christ ultimately meant being put to death. According to *Catechism of the Catholic Church*, "Martyrdom is the supreme witness given to the truth of the faith: it means bearing witness even unto death."[17]

---

14. James M. Nelson, *Psychology, Religion, and Spirituality* (New York: Springer Media, 2009), 427.
15. Li Nuo and Luisetta Mudie, "Chinese Christians Held in Secretive Brainwashing Camps: Sources," Radio Free Asia, www.rfa.org/english/news/china/christians-camps-04012021081013.html.
16. 3144. martus. *Strong's Greek Concordance*.
17. *Catechism of the Catholic Church*, Part III, Section II, Chapter II, Article 8, 2473.

YOU SHALL BE MY WITNESSES

Being a *witness* or *martyr* is not just reserved for those facing persecution. In fact, our Lord spoke of each of us being a witness and promised us power through the Holy Spirit.

> *You will receive power when the Holy Spirit has come upon you, and you will be my witnesses in Jerusalem and in all Judea and Samaria, and to the end of the earth.* (Acts 1:8)

A witness of Christ should always be ready to confess Him, by profession in word for all to hear of the faith, by keeping without compromise the commandments that He has given us, and by suffering to be mocked, despised, reviled, persecuted, and even put to the ultimate test—being a blood witness of Him, a martyr in the fullest sense. The consecration to martyrdom, so obviously shown in the persecuted, is an effect of the power of the Holy Spirit residing in us and an obligation which the body of Christ must be prepared to assume if called upon. In other words, it is the duty of every Christian to act as a witness of the gospel *no matter the cost*. This is perhaps the greatest lesson that Christians of the West have to learn from our persecuted brothers and sisters.

THE CHURCH'S RESPONSIBILITY TO PERSECUTED BELIEVERS

For centuries, the church took formal action to pray for and remember the persecuted and those who have been martyred for the faith. In fact, in Roman Catholicism, praying for the persecuted church was part of the daily and Sunday Masses. The *Roman Missal*—a book containing the prescribed prayers, chants, and instructions for the celebration of Mass in the Roman Catholic Church—includes specific instructions on how to pray for the persecuted and how to say a memorial mass for a saint who is inscribed in the martyrology for that specific day.[18] This means that the magisterium of the Roman Catholic Church formally concluded that it was important and necessary to pray for the suffering faithful and remember the martyred. The church's catechism says, "The Church has painstakingly collected the records of those who persevered to the end in witnessing

---

18. *The Roman Missal*, section 355b.

to their faith. These are the acts of the Martyrs. They form the archives of truth written in letters of blood."[19]

If this is all written in the formal teachings of the church, why has she lost her sense of responsibility and urgency toward the persecuted faithful? The answer is quite simple. Christians of the West have become an *inward focused* people. The Western church has lost its sense of responsibility for members of the body of Christ outside of their immediate community. For example, according to research conducted by the Traveling Team,[20] American Christians spend 95 percent of offerings on home-based ministry, 4.5 percent on cross-cultural efforts for already reached people groups, and 0.5 percent to reach the unreached. In other words, only 5 percent of donations from the American churches are being sent overseas, and most of that is going to people who already know Jesus.

There are no statistics available for how much specifically is going to aid the persecuted church, but one can speculate that it doesn't make up much of the 5 percent. These statistics are both shocking and telling, as they speak to the lack of care for our brothers and sisters abroad.

RECOVERING OUR CARE FOR THE PERSECUTED

What can we do? How do we recover our care for the persecuted? We first do so by holding fast to the words of Paul in Hebrews 13:3, "*Remember those who are in prison, as though in prison with them, and those who are mistreated, since you also are in the body.*" Each of us must make the continual commitment to actively call to mind the suffering members of the body of Christ. Secondly, we must make a commitment to *pray for the persecuted*. We often hear the expression, "There's nothing left to do but pray!" In reality, prayer should be the *first response* of any believer in any situation, especially when taking care of the body of Christ.

Throughout my travels to the Middle East and anytime I have had an opportunity to sit down with someone who has suffered for the sake

---

19. *Catechism of the Catholic Church*, 2473.
20. www.thetravelingteam.org.

of Christ, when I ask what they need most, they will almost always say, "Please continue to pray for us." This response shows us that the persecuted depend on our prayers for strength and solidarity. Furthermore, as believers we *know* that prayer has a powerful ability to bring change. Let us call upon our Father in heaven to send the Comforter to the persecuted, to bring conversion to the persecutors, and to continue to strengthen our brothers and sisters who risk their lives daily for the gospel.

Lastly, let us make the commitment to remember the martyrs and all those faithful witnesses who have, until their last breath, committed their lives to the gospel despite being mocked, despised, reviled, tortured, and, in many cases, put to death. As Pope John Paul II said in his homily on May 9, 2000, on the occasion of the Jubilee Pilgrimage of Romanians:

> Dear friends, preserve in your hearts the living memory of this martyrdom and pass it on to future generations so that it can continue to be a source of inspiration for a Christian witness that is always generous and authentic. Martyrdom is above all an intense spiritual experience: it flows from a heart that loves the Lord as the supreme truth and the greatest, indispensable good.[21]

---

21. www.vatican.va/content/john-paul-ii/en/homilies/2000/documents/hf_jp-ii_hom_20000509_romania.html.

17

RECOVERING OUR BATTLE AGAINST SIN

DAVID H. CAMPBELL

How often do we as believers struggle with the battle against sin in our lives? How can sin be an ever-present reality even in the lives of sincere Christians?

There is a tendency in much current preaching to inflate people's sense of worth and value in an attempt to make them feel good about themselves and their lives. Some teachers add to this the declaration that Christian believers are destined to be in a place of victory rather than always struggling through battles. Yet people continue to feel down about their circumstances and continue to experience adversity and apparent defeats.

When we present Christ as the quick and easy solution to all our problems, including sin, trouble is brewing. A gospel message focused on making people feel good about themselves by minimizing the ongoing reality of human fallenness is not much of a gospel at all. The solution lies in a recovery of the depth and meaning of our ongoing battle against sin. Only when we recover a true understanding of the battle can we move beyond moral platitudes and legalism toward a heart cry for help that recognizes our need for the grace of God. Otherwise, the battle is lost. Recovering an understanding of the depth of the battle, then, brings with it a recovery of our understanding of the grace of God that stands at the very heart of the gospel and the Christian life.

If we are going to figure out how to handle this issue well, we are going to navigate our way through Romans 7. There, Paul speaks of a man *"sold under sin"* (verse 14) who cannot succeed in doing what he wants, but rather does *"the very thing"* he hates (verse 15). Paul speaks in the first person singular as if he were speaking of himself. And more than that, he uses the personal pronoun *ego*, which makes the declaration emphatic: "It was *I* who once was alive…and it was *I* who died." (See Romans 7:9; the same emphatic form appears in verses 14, 20, 24, and 25.)

Augustine and Calvin set the stage for the classical understanding of this text, which holds that Paul was speaking as a believer of his own experience. But much modern interpretation, being unable to countenance the idea that a believer could experience such a battle against sin, has tended to deny this. Could it be that the weakening of our understanding of sin due to liberal, "woke" theology is behind this shift in interpretation? Such theology tends to relativize or even eliminate the reality of moral standards, and it guts the Bible of much of its teaching wherever that teaching tends to contradict the values pagan culture has embraced.

On a lighter but still sad note, consider the case of a long-ago member of my congregation who showed up one day to announce that after listening to some teaching, he had come to the conclusion not only that he had the capacity not to sin, but he was in fact now free from sin. I felt like taking him to the gym and dropping a weight on his toe to test how free from sin he was! His warped understanding of Scripture and his unwillingness to sit under the discipline of church leaders was sufficient evidence that he had not yet entirely escaped the clutches of the old nature.

Romans is a carefully planned letter. It is therefore unlikely that here in the midst of a sustained exposition of the Christian life, which takes place in chapters 5 through 8, we would have a portrait of the unbeliever practically unequalled in terms of depth and vividness anywhere in Paul's writings. It is a serious error to detach this passage from its wider context.

In Romans 5, Paul commences his description of Christian experience. Having declared in verse 21 that grace will *"reign though righteousness leading to eternal life through Jesus Christ our Lord,"* Paul must now make clear how this comes to fruition in the Christian life and how we must face the stumbling blocks to the attainment of Christian maturity. This he does in chapters 6–8. In chapter 6, the topic is dying to sin and the flesh through slavery to righteousness. Chapter 7 covers the flesh, sin, and God's law, while chapter 8 notes that living by the Holy Spirit will defeat the flesh and sin. *These are not three separate battles, but rather one conflict described from three different perspectives.*

Romans 6 deals with our death to sin. It has lots of past tenses that speak of our previous dying to sin. But notice also the string of present imperatives, starting with *"consider yourselves"* in verse 11, by which Paul exhorts his readers to put sin to death in their lives. In verse 12 he states, *"Let not sin therefore reign in your mortal body."* We find the same phenomenon in chapter 8. Like chapter 6, it begins with an affirmation that deliverance from sin is already accomplished. Yet only a few verses further on, we find this statement: *"So then, brothers, we are debtors, not to the flesh, to live according to the flesh"* (Romans 8:12). Believers live in a fallen world and must be exhorted continually to live according to the Spirit so that they do not lose the reality of a daily, living encounter with God, along with all the blessings this brings.

I look at it like this. You and I live in the world of the real. The real is where we are at in our walk with the Lord. We have gained some ground, as Paul writes in Philippians 3, but we have much more yet to cover. We are, to use Paul's example, runners running in a race. (See 1 Corinthians 9:24.) If where we are now is the real, then Christ Himself is the ideal. We're not there, but that is where we aim to be. Allow the ideal to pull you out of the real and toward Christ. Don't be complacent and don't compare yourself to others. All of us are falling short, but all of us who respond in obedience are being pulled forward by the grace of God toward the ideal, Jesus Himself. As long as you're moving forward, you're gaining ground. But to stand still is to fall back, for God's call is always toward Himself.

EXAMINING ROMANS 7 IN DETAIL

This shows us why the identity of the speaker in Romans 7 is a serious issue. Some cannot see a believer—in this case, the great apostle himself—admitting to such a level of sin still present in his own life. Yet orthodox Bible teaching has always insisted we must first take account of the depth of sinfulness within ourselves if we are to take hold of the resources to fight back. Trivializing sin or pretending it barely exists will do little to help us overcome it. The shallowness of many believers' experiences in our contemporary culture and the apparent ease with which many abandon the faith testify to the fact that the church has not adequately set out for us both the depths of our depravity without Christ and the seriousness of the battle in which we are still engaged as saved believers living in a fallen world that still affects us.

With this context in mind, let's take a look at the text. Remember that our goal here is to recover an understanding of the seriousness of sin and our need for the grace of God. Most commentators divide the section into two parts. The first part, verses 7–12, is characterized by use of the past tense. The second part, verses 13–23, is characterized almost completely by use of the present tense. Verses 24–25 bring a conclusion to the discussion.

Let's look at the opening paragraph first. A noteworthy feature of the entire chapter is the way in which Paul speaks in the first person singular. But who is he speaking about? In verse 9, he says that once he lived without the law. That couldn't possibly be Paul describing his own personal experience, for he was raised in the strictest practice of the law, *"circumcised on the eighth day, of the people of Israel, of the tribe of Benjamin, a Hebrew of Hebrews; as to the law, a Pharisee"* (Philippians 3:5).

The clue to the correct meaning lies in allusions Paul makes in the text to the story of the fall. The paragraph borrows terminology from Genesis to retell the story of Adam and Eve falling prey to the serpent. Sin (the serpent) seized *"an opportunity through the commandment"* (not to eat of the tree), *"deceived me"* (as the serpent deceived Eve), and *"killed me"* (verse 11). Paul uses the first person because he has just finished teaching that all of us fell in Adam. (See Romans 5:12–21.) And he goes on to connect God's commandment to Adam with the law later given to Moses. (See

Romans 5:14.) Because all of us are personally involved, Paul can speak as a representative of fallen humanity.

But if Paul is alluding to the fall, why then does he say, *"For I would not have known what it is to covet if the law had not said, 'You shall not covet'"* (Romans 7:7)? God said nothing to Adam about not coveting. Or did He? The commandment, "Do not covet" was closely linked by Jewish teachers to the story of the fall because of Eve's illegal desire for the forbidden fruit. The act of coveting was seen as summing up the whole expression of our sinfulness and rebellion against God in the garden. Sin found an opportunity in the commandment given in the garden not to eat the forbidden fruit. Through our disobedience, sin then was able to produce *"all kinds of covetousness"* in us (verse 8).

In verse 9, Paul again alludes to the account of Adam in the garden: *"I was once alive apart from the law, but when the commandment came, sin came alive and I died."* Only Adam could truly be said to have been fully *"alive"* before giving way to sin because sin first entered when Adam disobeyed the commandment. Then later, sin was clearly defined and multiplied through the law, as Romans 5:20–21 makes clear. *Paul is using the Genesis story to try to illustrate how sin uses a direct commandment, first with Adam and then later with the law, to increase its power over humanity.*

As any parent knows, the Genesis story is more than applicable to daily life. Try telling your four-year-old not to run into the road and see how many minutes pass before they attempt it. Or try telling them not to eat those cookies sitting on the counter when you leave the room. All the command does is focus their attention on satisfying their appetite as quickly as possible.

The commandment, which God intended to bring life, then actually brought death. (See Romans 7:10.) *"For sin, seizing an opportunity through the commandment, **deceived** me and through it killed me"* (verse 11). Here is another clear reference to Genesis, for the verb "deceived" alludes to the action of the serpent in regard to Eve. (See Genesis 3:13.) The commandment, which came from the mouth of God Himself, was not to blame. Neither, says Paul, can we say that the law, which also came from God, is to blame, and this is the bigger point he wants to make.

The enemy uses the good commands of the law to distort the purposes of God, to question His goodness, and to tempt us to rebel against Him. Yet the law itself is not to blame, for *"the law is holy, and the commandment is holy and righteous and good"* (Romans 7:12). We could take this a step further by saying that *neither is the gospel to blame* for the fact that it also is used by the enemy to incite rebellion in fallen humanity—indeed a greater rebellion, for this rebellion culminated in the crucifixion of the Son of God and continues today wherever in the world the crucified Savior is rejected and His followers are persecuted or killed.

Verses 7–12 show us that the law is good but has been used by the enemy for his own evil purposes. Verses 13–23 explain that it is sin, not the law, which leads to spiritual death. Contained within the second half of verse 13 are two clauses of purpose, both of which express a part of God's purpose in giving the law. He gave the law *"**in order that** sin might be recognized as sin, it used what is good to bring about my death, **so that** through the commandment sin might become utterly sinful"* (NIV). The law first uncovers the true reality of sin. Then, by challenging our rebellion, the law causes sin to be *"increased"*—that is *"become utterly sinful"*—in the hearts of those who rebel. (See Romans 5:20.) This does not express the entire purpose of God in giving the law. (See Romans 8:4.) The gospel has a similar but even greater effect than the law in that through the gospel events, the sin of humanity was so uncovered and enhanced that it led to the rejection and death of the God's own Son. Wherever in the world the gospel is preached, it often has the same effect. This was indeed part of the purpose of God in regard to the gospel, but clearly not the entire or even the main purpose. The same is true of the law.

Sin implants itself in us at a young age and is capable of exhibiting great ingenuity and creativity. Consider the case of my three-year-old grandson Ethan, who had listened intently to the Bible stories his parents had been reading to him at bedtime. The fruit of this great teaching experience was not quite what his mom expected. One day, she asked him to clean up after himself, and he replied, "No, thanks. I'm the prince of Sheba." A story about a rich ruler humbling himself before God had turned into an excuse for entitlement!

In Romans 7:14, Paul switches abruptly from the past tense to the present. Having described the events of the past in regard to the fall and the giving of the law, he now appears to be describing how these events are working themselves out in the present. We may ask the question we did earlier with regard to the statements in verses 7–13, "Of whom is Paul speaking?" He cannot be speaking of *himself prior to conversion*. That would not account for the continuous use of the *present* tense. But beyond that, Paul's own past as a self-righteous Pharisee, apparently blameless before God, is far removed from the picture here of a man deeply conscious of his own sinfulness. Neither, for the same reason, could he be speaking of *himself as representative of non-Christian Jews in general*, for Paul has presented them in chapter 2 as people certain of their own righteousness. And he could not be speaking of *himself as representative of humankind in general* as he was in verses 7–13, for this would be completely at odds with his presentation in Romans 1:18–32 of humanity's fallen state and complete disregard for the ways of God.

There is only one possibility left. *He must, therefore, be speaking of himself as a representative of the present experience of believers.* This is in line with the fact that chapters 1–3 speak of the life of unbelievers, while chapters 5–8 describe the Christian life. The fact that Paul describes his own experience this way underscores both the ongoing battle against sin and our desperate daily need for the power of the Holy Spirit to honor God and His commandments in our lives.

How could Paul describe himself as *"sold under sin"* (verse 14)? The closer we get to God, as godly Christians have testified through the ages, the more hopeless we realize our situation is without God's grace and the more awful appear our sin and rebellion. Of course, this must be taken in tension with chapter 8. The struggle of believers against sin and our overcoming by grace through the empowering of the Holy Spirit are *both* real aspects of the Christian life. Concentrating solely on the struggle against sin would lead us to despair but focusing only on overcoming by the Spirit would result in pride and a false sense of security.

How can Paul say he is *"sold under sin"* or *"I do the very thing I hate"* (verse 15)? While an unbeliever might have some occasional regret over their actions, it is unlikely, if they were otherwise in sound mind, that they would be pictured as hating their own moral choices and acts. But if the individual depicted here knows God and is indwelled by the Holy Spirit, has a deep consciousness of the chasm between God's righteousness and their own sinfulness, and is crying out to God for help in the battle against sin, the words spoken in verse 15 are entirely appropriate. The hatred of sin pictured in verse 15 can only come from the Holy Spirit who indwells us.

One of the most moving moments my wife and I have had in ministry occurred the day we were sitting with a ninety-three-year-old member of our congregation who was among the godliest people we ever knew. After a time of prayer, she confessed how much closer to the Lord she should be living and expressed her hope that the Lord would mercifully draw her to Himself in a deeper way.

To acknowledge our lack is not to deny the work God has done in our lives. Instead, it kick starts a cry for help that only God's grace can give to draw us the rest of the way.

In Romans 7:16, Paul says that his failure to meet God's standard the way he wants to shows that he agrees *"with the law, that it is good."* Only Christian believers truly align themselves with God's law. The gentile unbeliever would not acknowledge the law at all. The Jewish unbeliever, while acknowledging the law, would not agree that the law itself shows up the darkest recesses of sin in their heart. But Paul states, *"I have the desire to do what is right, but not the ability to carry it out"* (verse 18). He does not mean he cannot do anything at all, but that whatever he does *never fully accomplishes what he desires*. He sees the perfect will of God but cannot reach it on his own.

In verse 21, Paul begins to draw some conclusions from the preceding verses. Paul is saying that his experience proves that when he turns to do good, sin stands in the way. Yet he goes on to say he delights in God's law (verse 22). To delight in the law is surely the cry of the sincere believer. This rejoicing occurs in the *"inner being,"* that deep place in the believer's heart where the Holy Spirit works. The sentence is concluded in verse 23, *"But I see in my members another law waging war against the law of my mind and making me captive to the law of sin that dwells in my members."* In verses 22–23, two laws are pictured at war with each other. The *"law of sin"* is waging war against the *"law of my mind."* The first law represents the power or control exercised over us by sin. The *"law of my mind"* is the *"law of God"* in verse 22.

Is it possible that such a war could occur within the life of the Spirit-filled believer? The answer must surely be yes. Indeed, it is *only* within the believer that the war is waged. There is no such battle going on in the unbeliever, who does not even acknowledge God's law or claim on his life. But within the believer, the battle has been joined. (See Romans 6:12.) The battle is fierce, but the eventual outcome, as chapter 8 shows us, is not in doubt.

The last two verses of Romans 7 form a conclusion to all that Paul has said in verses 7–23. The speaker acknowledges his condition. He serves sin in his flesh but God in his mind. Yet God will surely deliver him. Through his use of the first person singular and the present tense, Paul is expressing in these verses both the struggle that he faces personally in his own battle against sin and the struggle he knows is real in the heart of every believer. To ignore or deny the existence of such a struggle betrays a deception as to the measure of our own sanctification, or even perhaps the presence of a legalistic spirit.

You and I live in what I call the great in-between. How do we live in that tension of being in the real while being drawn toward the ideal? One key, I think, is always to be grateful for the grace that has brought us thus far, yet always wanting and needing more to take us home. In that passage in Philippians 3 where Paul talks about pressing on toward the prize, he says, *"I do not consider that I have made it my own"* (verse 13). The word "consider" is borrowed from the world of accounting and means to "reckon." A businessman friend of mine had a prosperous hardware business, but the time of year he hated most was when he had to close to take inventory. It was tedious, and he made no sales. But it was necessary. We need to stop and take inventory from time to time. We need to invite our spouse or trusted friends to help us in our task. Where have we made progress and can rejoice? Where do we need to improve? This is not spiritual self-help; it is simply an acknowledgement of where we're at, which gives us the motivation to cry out to God for the grace which alone can bring change into our lives.

The battle for freedom is fought on the basis of the work of Christ. The outcome of the battle is certain. Yet in the meantime, the battle persists and can only be fought by the empowering of the Spirit. Toward the end of World War II, Allied forces landed in Normandy, an event known as D-Day. The war did not end until Victory in Europe Day almost a year later. Many battles were fought, and many casualties occurred between those two days. But from D-Day onward, the outcome was determined.

We live in the great in between, between the day of Jesus's resurrection and the day of His final return. There are battles to fight, many of which will not be easy, yet the outcome is assured. So even in the midst of battle, we can join with Paul in looking forward confidently to the deliverance awaiting us in Christ, and with him declare, *"Thanks be to God through Jesus Christ our Lord!"* (Romans 7:25).

18

RECOVERING THE WAY WE LEARN

COREY O'NEILL

In the summer of 2021, my wife and I visited Goat Hill Overlook, where George Washington spied on the British from across the Delaware River. As we enjoyed the view, a family of four joined us—two parents and two small children. One of the children, of preschool age, saw a sign that read "Goat Hill Overlook" and was met with an educational stumbling block. She asked, "Mommy, what does that say?" Mommy told her the answer and gave her a pack of Dunkaroos.

I'm kidding. Actually, Mommy turned the moment into an opportunity for her daughter to learn. She had her spell it by herself with letters of the alphabet that, presumably, she had already been taught. The American Fabius himself would've been proud.

The following year, I enrolled in Theos Seminary, where I too was challenged by a phrase: *tohu va-vohu*. The assignment was a research paper on this Hebrew word-pair found in Genesis 1:2. Even though researching *tohu va-vohu* was more appropriate for my age than *spelling* it would have been, I struggled.

Why? I suppose the same can be asked of the minister whose theology hasn't developed in ten years, or of the longtime congregant who doesn't know that he has a theology to develop. What has happened to the way we learn? Clearly, we lose it at some point after we figure out how to spell.

Recovery will demand more than behavior modification. Applying the right study habits and reading the right books won't solve the student's problem any more than switching to beer or drinking only on weekends will solve the alcoholic's problem. Physician William D. Silkworth once said, "Unless [the alcoholic] can experience an entire psychic change, there is very little hope for his recovery."[1]

The aim of this essay is an entire psychic change—the dismantling and replacing of certain beliefs regarding the way we learn.

This can't be achieved without first understanding modern education's reimagining of the student. In *The Rise and Triumph of the Modern Self*, Carl R. Trueman explores a concept called the *social imaginary*, which shows us how *anything* can be reimagined. Drawing on the works of philosopher Charles Taylor, he writes, "The social imaginary…refers to the myriad beliefs, practices, normative expectations, and even implicit assumptions that members of a society share and that shape their daily lives. It is not so much a conscious philosophy of life as a set of intuitions and practices."[2] Where do these intuitions come from? According to Taylor, "Theory is often the possession of a small minority."[3] Societal norms, therefore, are usually the philosophies not of the masses, but of the elite who have the means to influence the masses.

When it comes to implicit assumptions about students, one example I think of is *senioritis*, that infectious disease that causes high school students to give up on learning, usually once junior year ends. Everyone

---

1. Alcoholics Anonymous World Services Inc., "The Doctor's Opinion," in *Alcoholics Anonymous*, 4th ed. (New York City: Alcoholics Anonymous World Services, Inc., 2001), xxix.
2. Carl R. Trueman, *The Rise and Triumph of the Modern Self: Cultural Amnesia, Expressive Individualism, and the Road to Sexual Revolution* (Wheaton, IL: Crossway, 2020).
3. Ibid.

expects it, so everyone accepts it. After all, they've already gotten into college, where they'll care about learning again. Though senioritis isn't the topic of this essay, exploring its origin will help us recover the way we learn.

Our social imaginary—our implicit assumptions and practices—pertaining to students didn't get here overnight. Norms like *senioritis* trace back to the social efficiency movement of the early twentieth century. Jonghun Kim writes that in the United States, European immigrants "did not only contribute to the further expansion of the industrial economy, but also caused an explosion of the student population in schools."[4] According to Kim, efficiency was paramount during this time, and non-English speaking people "were regarded as 'threats' to social progress, thereby raising the need to control and manage them."[5] For the sake of America's efficiency, means of controlling and managing them took place in schools. This required the reimagining of the student, which would undermine *how* and *why* we learn.

Before the student could be reimagined, schools and teachers had to be reimagined. This was accomplished, according to Kim, via mechanical engineer Frederick Winslow Taylor's theory of scientific management or Taylorism, which "refers to management techniques aimed at maximizing productivity in the manufacturing industry."[6] Taylor's methods of reducing the time and cost of manufacturing were translated to classrooms—and to say that this affected education would be an understatement.

University instructor John Franklin Bobbitt was an outspoken proponent of schools adopting Taylorism. His work on this matter is telling regarding what role he believed teachers were to play. He wrote:

> The burden of finding the best methods is too large and too complicated to be laid on the shoulders of the teachers…The ultimate

---

4. Jonghun Kim, "School accountability and standard-based education reform: The recall of social efficiency movement and scientific management," *International Journal of Educational Development*, vol. 60, May 2018, 80–87.
5. Ibid.
6. Ibid.

worker, the teacher in our case, must be a specialist in the performance of the labour that will produce the product.⁷

Bobbit likened education specialists to *factory managers*, teachers to *laborers*, schools to *assembly lines*, and students to *products*. None of these had ever been imagined this way, but once the inefficiency of schools forecasted the inefficiency of America's economy, Taylorism's proponents stepped in and changed the institutions of the masses. This led to the advent of the standardized test. Thus, a new assumption was added to our social imaginary: the student who memorizes the most learns the most.

This reimagining of the student has led to what Kim calls "the dehumanization in schooling."⁸ According to Wayne Au, standardized testing is a major perpetrator of this, as teachers are pressured to teach to the test.⁹ Their autonomy over the classroom has been stripped away, diminishing their relationship with the students. Ultimately, students are robbed of the ability to know their teachers. The person they see next to the dry-erase board isn't the teacher, but merely a facilitator.

Now this essay isn't about recovering public education. I *do* intend to offer a way to recover the way we learn. In light of what I've discussed so far, we lose the way we learn much like an alcoholic loses control over his life: by living in a cycle for many years. For students, that cycle is:

- We begin learning for the sake of being *efficient*.
- We spend our time as students learning *efficiently*.
- We stop learning once *efficiency* has given us what we want.

Efficiency is necessary for manufacturing, but is it good for *learning*? G. K. Chesterton, a critic of social efficiency, didn't think so. In *Heretics*, he wrote:

> When everything about a people is for the time growing weak and ineffective, it begins to talk about efficiency. So it is that when a

---

7. John Franklin Bobbitt, *The supervision of city schools: the twelfth yearbook of the national society for the study of education* (Bloomington, IL: Public School Pub., 1913), 52–53, quoted in Wayne Au, "Teaching Under the New Taylorism: High-Stakes Testing and the Standardization of the 21st Century Curriculum," *Journal of Curriculum Studies* 43:1, February 1, 2011, 25–45.
8. Kim, "School accountability and standard-based education reform".
9. Au, "Teaching Under the New Taylorism".

man's body is a wreck he begins, for the first time, to talk about health. Vigorous organisms talk not about their processes, but about their aims. There cannot be any better proof of the physical efficiency of a man than that he talks cheerfully of a journey to the end of the world. And there cannot be any better proof of the practical efficiency of a nation than that it talks constantly of a journey to the end of the world, a journey to the judgment day and the New Jerusalem.[10]

What are the aims of twenty-first century students? If they have aims, they often revolve around earning a paycheck. This is our social imaginary—our subconsciously-held assumptions about learning, shaped by the consciously-held philosophies of elitists who have lost sight of why formation is important.

We would do well to consider why the ancients became students. The word *school* took on an entirely different meaning in antiquity than it does today, which helps us understand how Greeks and Romans viewed the school and the teacher.

Ansgar Allen explains:

> [School] derives from the Greek term *scholē*, which signified leisure, rest and idleness, learned discussion, or a place where leisure and discussion might take place. In classical Latin, the related *schola* is more didactic in sense, referring to the exposition of a teacher of their views on a subject or to the place or establishment where a teacher expounds.[11]

Does the modern student enjoy leisure and discussion in class? Is the modern educator expected to know a subject well enough to teach it from the heart? Generally speaking, no. In fact, modern educators would sneer at the seeming inefficiency of the Greeks and Romans, *who would sneer back.* To them, becoming a student was less about working at the widget

---

10. G. K. Chesterton, "Introductory Remarks on the Importance of Orthodoxy," in *Heretics* (New Kensington, PA: Whitaker House, 2013), 8–9.
11. Ansgar Allen, "Ancient Schools and the Challenge of Cynicism," in Avi I. Mintz, ed., *A History of Western Philosophy of Education in Antiquity* vol. 1 (London, Bloomsbury Publishing, 2021), 147.

factory than it was about developing a certain way of life.[12] Their aim was to "furnish the aristocracy with men who were considered both beautiful and good."[13]

Surely, the ancient Greeks and Romans can help us recover, right? Not exactly. The education we need comes from a teacher who long precedes the ancients—the one who came into the world, was born of a virgin in Bethlehem, and effectively reimagined the student, the teacher, the school, the beautiful, and the good.

Indeed, Taylorism wasn't the first pedagogy or method of teaching to reimagine education. That role in history belongs to Christianity. Yun Lee Too affirms this; his comparison of Augustine as a teacher before and after his conversion strangely makes Christian pedagogy seem like Taylorism—but there's one crucial difference. He says, "Augustine is no longer the teacher but rather the facilitator of teaching, which occurs through Christ."[14]

Both Christianity and Taylorism made the teacher a facilitator, but only Christianity made the teacher omnipresent and omniscient. This teacher freely expounds His views, while His students enjoy leisure, rest, and discussion. This isn't another social imaginary, where the philosophies of the elitists shape the intuitions of the masses. Here, the body of Christ has the same philosophy as the Head, who forms His students in ways that are impossible for the human teacher.

This prestigious, heavenly university has had multitudes of students, yet many still lose the way they learn. According to a 2018 Barna study, only 10 percent of those eighteen to twenty-nine years old who grew up as Christians are resilient disciples.[15] These are "Christ followers who (1) attend church at least monthly and engage with their church more than just attending worship services; (2) trust firmly in the authority of the Bible; (3) are committed to Jesus personally and affirm

---

12. Ibid.
13. Ansgar Allen and Roy Goddard, *Education & Philosophy: An Introduction* (Los Angeles: SAGE Publications, 2017).
14. Yun Lee Too, "St. Augustine's Pedagogy as the New Creation," in Mintz's *A History of Western Philosophy of Education in Antiquity*, 236.
15. David Kinnaman and Mark Matlock, *Faith for Exiles: 5 Ways for a New Generation to Follow Jesus in Digital Babylon* (Grand Rapids, MI: Baker Publishing Group, 2019).

he was crucified and raised from the dead to conquer sin and death; and (4) express desire to transform the broader society as an outcome of their faith."[16]

For every ten young adults who grew up having the greatest teacher in the universe, only one of them has learned from Him. What happened to the other nine? I propose that they aren't resilient disciples for the same reason why we've *all* lost the way we learn: in our social imaginary, we've lost sight of why we should become students. In the ancient world, it was to be good people. In modern society, it's to be efficient people. However, Christians should study to become efficient and good at loving God and other people.

Becoming a student for this purpose will recover the way we learn. All other motives will prevent recovery. Surely, this has been our trouble since the fall of man. In the final chapter of the Epistle to Diognetus, the author comments on how mankind's loveless pursuit of knowledge ironically robbed him of knowledge. He then quotes Scripture to reveal the key to recovery:

> God in the beginning planted "a tree of knowledge and a tree of life in the midst of Paradise," and showed that life is through knowledge. But those who did not use it in purity were in the beginning deprived of it by the deceit of the serpent; for neither is there life without knowledge, nor sound knowledge without true life; wherefore both are planted together. And when the apostle saw the force of this, he blamed the knowledge which is exercised apart from the truth of the injunction which leads to life and said; "Knowledge puffeth up, but love edifieth."[17]

Learning that is divorced from the love of God puffs up the student with the *illusion* of knowledge. Such is the conviction of both the author of this epistle and Paul, who reproached the early church at Corinth for their misuse of knowledge to justify eating food sacrificed to idols:

---

16. Ibid.
17. Pope Clement I et al., *The Apostolic Fathers*, ed. Kirsopp Lake, vol. 2, The Loeb Classical Library (Cambridge MA; London: Harvard University Press, 1912–1913), 377–379.

> Now concerning food offered to idols: we know that "all of us possess knowledge." This "knowledge" puffs up, but love builds up. If anyone imagines that he knows something, he does not yet know as he ought to know. (1 Corinthians 8:1–2)

Traditionally, this chapter is interpreted as Paul's response to whether the Corinthians may knowingly eat idol food, but this misses the point.[18] Paul had already forbidden them to do so, and 1 Corinthians 8 is him telling them why.[19] He will correct their theology about idols in verse five, for they believed that there were no gods but God. He assures them that there *are* evil entities involved in these sacrifices, and a Christian can't knowingly eat idol food in a neutral manner.[20]

Still, there is a deeper issue that Paul's addressing in verses 1–2: the way they're learning. Correcting their theology wasn't enough to recover it. That the Corinthians wished to knowingly eat idol food is indicative of a missing component to their learning: the love of God. Without it, they were artificially puffed up, rather than spiritually built up. They possessed knowledge about the supremacy of Christ and their freedom in Him, but that wasn't enough. Of the student who considers head knowledge alone to be knowledge, Paul says, *"he does not yet know as he ought to know."*

How then, ought we to know? In his commentary on this passage, David E. Garland tells us how: "Believers must understand fully the broad sweep of theological implications and let their conduct be leavened with love."[21] The student of Christ can't have knowledge without love and expect to recover the way he learns. He will be no more formed than the student under Taylorism. He may pencil in every right answer on the test, but he still knows nothing. Knowing the way he ought to know can only be achieved under Augustine's pedagogy. This means that formation extends beyond classrooms, Bible studies, and Sunday services. It must also occur in the silent, secret place, where the Holy Spirit forms Christ in us.[22]

---

18. David E. Garland, *1 Corinthians: Baker Exegetical Commentary on the New Testament* (Grand Rapids, MI: Baker Publishing Group, 2003).
19. Ibid.
20. Ibid.
21. Ibid.
22. Too, "St. Augustine's Pedagogy as the New Creation".

Let me offer a hypothetical story about learning being recovered. You're a second-year seminary student living at home with your parents and your brother. It's the day before Labor Day, which means your church's youth pastor finally gets to preach on a Sunday. Dad, knowing ahead of time that Pastor Chad is preaching, fakes a migraine and stays home. So you, your mom, and your brother go to church and hear a message about being a child of God.

Dad doesn't enjoy his free time as much as he thought he would. The conviction of the Holy Spirit is so strong that he doesn't even have the appetite for burgers and dogs later. He knows that he sinned, and he knows that God knows. Suddenly, he hears from the Holy Spirit, *"For the Lord disciplines the one he loves, and chastises every son whom he receives"* (Hebrews 12:6). Dad asks for forgiveness, tunes in to the end of Pastor Chad's sermon on Facebook Live, and engages in the comments.

The rest of the family is on their way home. Mom is reciting every sermon point she wrote in her notebook…because she only learns from sermons. Your brother is deconstructing his faith…because he only learns from other deconstructionists. You're judging every heathen you drive past who went to brunch instead of church…because you've learned nothing at seminary. Apparently, the only person in this family who learned what it means to be a child of God that day is the one who stayed home.

This story is fictitious, but the characters are real. They're the Pentecostals who only learn from other Pentecostals, or the Calvinists who only learn from other Calvinists. They're the pro-abortion pastor and the longtime congregant who brings her unbelieving neighbor to Sunday service so that someone else can articulate the gospel to him.

All of them would do well to abandon Taylorism, where learning occurs on man's terms, and sit under Augustine's pedagogy, where learning occurs on *God's* terms.

How? I suggest repeating this three-step cycle to *recover* the way we learn:

1. *Begin learning in paradox.* Approach learning like all wise men do, with the realization that the more you know, the more you

don't know. This will open the door for important revelation from people with whom you disagree.

2. *Continue learning in silence.* Don't compartmentalize your learning. Your Teacher is omnipresent and omniscient. When you learn something new, allow that revelation to develop by meditating on it and praying about it.

3. *Finish learning in love.* God teaches to the test, but His tests *actually* prove whether you're learning, or whether you're merely memorizing. They're life's opportunities to either walk in the Spirit, or to walk in the flesh. Seek to score well not to be a teacher's pet, but to learn more from Him because you love Him.

Under these principles, the single mother who hasn't the time or the money for TheosU has an opportunity to receive the highest quality of education available; she may even learn more than the Theos Seminary student! *And she will bear fruit that remains.* (See John 15:16.)

You see, when an alcoholic recovers, he isn't the only person whose life improves. His wife, his children, and even other alcoholics benefit from his recovery. Likewise, when we as students recover the way we learn, the ripple effect has no limits.

19

RECOVERING CHRIST AS KING

NATHAN FINOCHIO

I learned how to golf with my friends who don't golf. This was before the Internet—in the 1990s, when you had to read a book (no thanks), pay for lessons (I was broke), have a friend who was a pro (I was from a blue-collar community, so fat chance), or be extraordinarily gifted (lol definitely not). So I golfed like a baseball player because baseball is the pastime of the plebeians. Sidenote: naming your daughter Patricia is a bit self-congratulatory.

Baseball players just swing with little or no form, and they swing "across" the ball, mainly just trying to make connection, seeing as there is a tiny ball speeding toward them in an uncertain direction.

Golf looks like it should be infinitely easier. After all, the ball is on a tee—it isn't even moving. And this is how dummies like me approach golf.

"It's like tee-ball—just hit the ball."

And this is why I was an atrocious golfer for decades, particularly off the tees. I had this baseball swing that resulted in a consistent slice. The other boys would bomb one off the tee, and I'd be setting up facing 45 degrees from the fairway; I'd play to my slice, and the ball would go 180 yards, somewhere near the fairway and well behind everyone else.

I had a love-hate relationship with golf. I loved hanging with the boys but hated golfing because I never learned how to swing properly.

Two years ago, everything changed.

I was golfing with a large group of friends in Palm Desert, California, at the JW Marriott golf course. It was an off-season day, and the course was wide open. There were probably about nine of us playing as one group. One of the guys was a preacher friend of mine who is an insanely talented golfer. As everyone was hitting their tee shot, I confessed to my friend that my drive was garbage.

"I keep slicing."

"Show me your swing," he replied.

I swung.

He said, "Okay, so what you're doing is coming across the ball, and that's why the ball is slicing. At the top of your swing, I want you to make a tiny U shape with your club head and pull the club head inside of the U on the way down. That should change the trajectory of the club from coming across the ball and make it come down straight. Most of the guys on the tour do some form of a U-shape swing."

I tried it a couple times in practice.

Stepped up to the tee box.

Stuck my tee in the ground and placed my ball on top.

Addressed the ball. Did a U at the top of my swing, just like my friend said.

And the ball went straight as an arrow, 250 yards down the fairway.

The group applauded. I had my man card back.

How you learn something matters.

My concern for Millennials and Gen Z is how they are learning Christ. It's like they're trying to play golf as if it's tee-ball. No one is teaching them the trajectory that will lead them to the hole-in-one that is Jesus Christ, our King, Lord, and Savior.

Paul had the same concern for some of the Ephesians, and he has this to say:

> *Now this I say and testify in the Lord, that you must no longer walk as the Gentiles do, in the futility of their minds. They are darkened in their understanding, alienated from the life of God because of the ignorance that is in them, due to their hardness of heart. They have become callous and have given themselves up to sensuality, greedy to practice every kind of impurity. But that is not the way you learned Christ!—assuming that you have heard about him and were taught in him, as the truth is in Jesus.* (Ephesians 4:17–21)

The gentiles had a cultural way of thinking. Paul says their way of thinking alienated them from the life of God because it hardened their hearts toward the gospel. But that was not how the Ephesians learned Christ. They *heard* and were *taught* the *truth* about following Jesus.

Paul continues:

> *You were taught, with regard to your former way of life, to put off your old self, which is being corrupted by its deceitful desires; to be made new in the attitude of your minds; and to put on the new self.* (Ephesians 4:22–24 NIV)

These Ephesians were taught a Christianity that requires a *putting off* of their old self and a *putting on* of their new self. This is how they *"learned Christ."* Let me rephrase it: this was their introduction to the gospel. It wasn't a class they heard five years later. It wasn't a one-on-one conversation they had after being in the church for four years. They were fully aware of what they were signing up for from day one.

Paul's gospel is summarized in Romans 1, so if we wonder what people heard as an introduction to Christ, it's that humanity has carnal issues for which they must repent and exchange for the life of God in Christ Jesus. Identity markers and practices that defined people's existence or consumed their thoughts and actions were challenged from day one, and thus they had a decision to make: choose salvation through Christ—which meant agreeing with God about their issue and partnering with the powerful grace of God toward them—or hardening their heart toward Christ because of how consumed and given over they were to their carnal practices.

I lived in New York City for eight years and attended a soul-winning church where I led worship for four years and eventually became a teaching pastor for another four years. We saw over 200,000 responses to presentations of what I believed (at the time) was the gospel message: Jesus loves you, died for you, and wants a relationship with you. God wants to be a part of your life; He brought you here today and wants to make everything new.

And that is most of the message—but it leaves out vital details that set the pace for the relationship between us and God.

First, you are a sinner, and your sins deserve death—in fact, hell.

Second, Jesus had to die in order to pay the price of your sins. Your sins cost Jesus dearly. He was beaten and whipped and suffered because of them.

Third, we have to *"repent and be baptized"* (Acts 2:38)—the dominant theme of the New Testament.

If that's not in a gospel presentation, can we really call it a gospel presentation? Because that's the most basic and consistent content that Jesus and the apostles presented.

See, if you don't see yourself as a sinner and rather just as a broken person who God thinks is adorable and wants to help make successful, famous, and virtuous, you're gonna begin to have all kinds of problems with Scripture and ultimately God. The relationship has to begin on the right note—that God is holy and has a problem with sin, and He graciously and mercifully dealt with it at the cross in the person and work of Christ. And the Scriptures have to be seen as the authority on the gospel, not as an ancient book that is problematic and needs to be glossed over because all of your instincts are perfect and pure, and you don't need to be anyone except yourself.

I have a suspicion that the seeker movement has profoundly damaged the gospel, and in its virtuous attempt to make the church a welcoming and culturally palatable experience, it has sanitized foundational elements of the message of Christ. The result, I believe, has been catastrophic. Because we haven't made disciples but rather *"decisions"*—and decisions for what, I ask? Decisions have no root.

There are many young people who *got saved* at our church, plugged into serving on teams and attending connect groups, worshipped with tears, sang the songs, took the notes, said *amen* at all the right times, and are now deconstructing into total apostasy.

The deconstruction movement is quite a large umbrella, and there are many entry points. You have ordained Christian pastors who preached every Sunday at evangelical churches, wrote Christian books, and preached at conferences…who are now divorced, agnostic, and living in Canada. Or you have former Christian musical artists who are now loud, proud atheists, not just quiet and passive about their crisis but leading others into apostasy. With their active unbelief, they *"suppress the truth"* (Romans 1:18).

I pray that God grants them repentance.

Then there are people who never had roots. They aren't really deconstructing because there was never anything there to tear down. They enjoyed being part of a community; they liked the sermons about how God is obsessed with them. They felt good about themselves when they went to church and learned lessons about life and relationships that were insightful and practical. They didn't feel so lonely during those days.

And this is why we need to recover what a gospel presentation is.

The parable of the sower has been really messing with me as I have contemplated all of the hands raised and the question, "Where are they now?" Are they Christians? Or are they in for a surprise on the day of judgment? God forbid. I want to believe that they are granted paradise and eternal life. But I worry when I read the New Testament. And I wonder if I've been to blame in the past because I was part of the problem.

In Matthew 13:3–8 and 13:18–23, Jesus describes a sower who was throwing seed everywhere, almost indiscriminately. Some of the seed fell on the path and was eaten up by birds. Jesus says the path represents a person who doesn't understand the word that was preached, and the devil comes and eats up that good seed.

The sower scattered some seed in rocky places where there was no deep soil, and though the seed sprang up quickly, when the sun came, the plant got scorched and withered because it had no root. Jesus explains that the rocky ground typifies people who hear and receive the word quickly *"with joy,"* but because they have no root—no discipleship—when hard times come, they quickly fall away.

Some other seed fell among thorns but the growth was stinted and ultimately choked. This refers to someone who hears the word, *"but the cares of the world and the deceitfulness of riches choke the word, and it proves unfruitful"* (verse 22). These people need to be famous more than they need to be saved, so they sacrifice being obedient to the word in exchange for the glory of being welcomed by Hollywood. Or if they identify with a Christ who demands repentance, it will hurt them financially, so they abort a child or take a public position contrary to Scripture, making Jesus out to be an unmerciful tyrant and a liar.

But the seed that fell on the good soil and became fruitful is typified as one who hears the gospel, understands it, is discipled in it, has roots, and sticks with Jesus no matter what it costs them.

These people are called Christians.

They aren't perfect—far from it. They make mistakes—lots of them. They still deal with sin and rebellion and have to constantly repent of all kinds of things. They are always in process.

But they are committed to Jesus over anything else.

When they come to a passage in the New Testament that they don't like, they assume that the Bible is right, and they are wrong. They aren't a self-authority. Jesus isn't their life coach with some great pointers but a couple total duds; Jesus is Lord and His Word is to be agreed with and obeyed. And when Christians regularly fall short, they ask the Holy Spirit for power to conform to the image of the Son.

They don't abandon Jesus.

They refuse to abandon Jesus.

That's lordship—and it's super old school. Yeah, it's the least sexy teaching in churches, but it's what fulfills the Great Commission.

Problematically, we have a lot of people in our churches who don't understand the gospel or the Bible because our preachers have copied forms and not learned theology. They love the messages and language of their heroes, who are also confused. And so they just employ unclear terminology that never comes close to announcing to a crowd that they are sinners, as Jesus regularly did. Confused preachers make statements that mean nothing and everything.

I often get asked by people on social media to give a statement on the vapid musings of so-and-so. It's really difficult to nail them down; I can't really tell what they are saying because *they* don't know what they are saying. Their congregations seem to know exactly what they are saying, which is the irony. You can ask a congregant what the preacher said and get one version but ask the preacher later, and they say something entirely different behind closed doors.

It's dishonest, crowd-pleasing politicking. And I suppose in some ways, it's genius. Because the priest is for hire and the prophet prophesies for a price. And it works for them.

But it doesn't accomplish what needs to be accomplished, which is helping people understand the cost of following Jesus.

Then there's the problem of the root, or total lack thereof.

Discipleship is lifelong, but we need practices and methods of discipleship that aren't just organic. We need classes, schools, and intentional plans to take our people through the Scriptures. We need to explain the Scriptures to them. We need to teach them how to read and why some ways are helpful while others are not.

I'm not suggesting that Sunday morning needs to be where we are doing all the heavy lifting either. But we need more than four weeks of an introduction to a church, small groups, and serving.

By creating a root system, we are helping people understand and know what Christ is asking of them—and who is the Christ making these demands. Because Jesus doesn't just tell us to be perfect and then peace out. He gives us the Holy Spirit, who empowers us, leads us, and guides us. The Holy Spirit has given us the Scriptures, and the Holy Spirit does miracles. He destroys strongholds, breaks heavy yokes, and sets people free from things that bound them for years.

If I don't know what God is capable of, I will feel overwhelmed by the task of Christianity. The point of the root is to show people who God has been and is and will be, to encourage them against the giants in the promised land and remind them that God will fight battles for us if we remain faithful witnesses to His goodness and glory.

The love of the world is absolutely the major issue with deconstruction.

When we come to Jesus and Scripture, we aren't nobodies from nowhere with nothing to offer. We come to Jesus and the Bible having been fully formed (or conformed) people, shaped intellectually, culturally, morally, politically, and socially with a complete worldview. We aren't blank slates; we are individuals who are a product of secular humanism and have a sense of what is right or wrong that was given to us by the architects of our society.

No one has an original sense of right and wrong; we've learned it mimetically from our friends, our favorite teacher, our beloved movie, our cherished entertainers, and the pop songs that have become our battle hymns. We are human sponges that collect values, many of which have become subconscious.

If our dad was a hardworking entrepreneur who taught us the value of sweat equity, capitalism would be our knee-jerk of what is fair. If our dad was a truck driver who was injured in an accident, never compensated properly, and struggling with health issues, thus impacting the family finances, our intuition would be that business owners are snakes and socialism is the answer to the problems facing the modern family.

This happens with every issue, particularly on social issues, and even more so if you have friends or family who are involved. Empathy has become the highest moral good; if you disagree with someone who is having an experience, you are an evil person. There is no right and wrong, only someone's experience.

So when we come to Scripture and we see Jesus absolutely trashing casual divorce, but we have friends who have divorced casually and remarried, it becomes a major crisis of faith. We think, *How could I possibly take sides against my divorced friends? That would make me a cruel, unsympathetic friend.*

In the cult of empathy, the first thing to go is often Scripture. Once Scripture goes, the whole thing has to go. Rebellion begets rebellion. Jesus is no longer Lord, because if He's not Lord of all, He's not Lord at all.

Jesus has to be Lord of the things we don't like. That's His prerogative. As King, He gets to make the rules.

This is the first principle of the gospel. Jesus makes the rules.

And if you don't learn Christ as King, you don't experience Christ as Savior.

20

RECOVERING MYSTERY

CHRIS PALMER

"I want my money back."

This is my own quote. I muttered it the day I graduated from Bible college.

After four years of study, I'd come no closer to clarifying Christianity's great mysteries. The Trinity hurt my brain. The hypostatic union had me tongue-tied. Premillenialism, postmillenialism, or amillennialism? I was a ballroom dancer taking turns to waltz with each maiden.

Not saying I didn't learn anything. I could slice up Greek words finer than a slap-chop and pontificate through every clause of the Nicene Creed like I'd been to the fourth century and back. And, well, I suppose I could write a sermon fair enough to keep a few people awake for forty-five minutes.

But I had come for the big stuff.

The gut punch came after my first year of ministry. It dawned on me how many times I'd had to tell a congregant, "I don't know."

I worked as a pastoral care minister in inner-city Detroit. Five days a week, I made my rounds to local hospitals, visiting sick saints. It wasn't unusual for me to have an initial patient visit and officiate at that person's funeral a few weeks or months later.

In one instance, twenty-five-year-old Allison asked me to visit her mother, which I did. A month later, Allison's mother died in the slow agony of stomach cancer. Pictures by her casket showed how beautiful she was during her vibrant life.

Allison found me after the service. "Minister Palmer, thank you for the warm eulogy. My family was comforted. Could I ask you a sincere question?"

I braced myself. I knew what was coming. I'd heard this question ten times before that moment, and I've heard it a hundred times since.

"Why did God let my mom die?"

At lot was at stake. All wrapped into a single question about the fate of a loved one.

"I don't know, Allison." In those days, I was uncomfortable using those three words, "I don't know."

Conservative Protestantism had been my hermeneutical location—the place from which I found myself interpreting Scripture. By default, I inherited my environment's approach to the text. Conservative Protestants, whether they realize it or not, approach Scripture like a book of hard facts. Historically, they have relied on the Baconian scientific method to approach the mysteries we read about in the Bible, just as one approaches the mysteries of science.

Sir Francis Bacon, one of the founders of modern science, promoted inductive reasoning and direct observation for scientific investigation. His ideas grew popular in the nineteenth century and were seen as a means for advancing theology. Baconianism had a *ruthless* emphasis on scientific facts and evidence. It was antitheoretical and empirical. C. Leonard Allen notes that Protestants used Baconianism to build harmony between natural science, the Christian faith, and morality. "By this means they believed that all knowledge—whether scientific, theological, or moral—could be placed upon a sure foundation."[1]

Today, fundamentalist Christians, particularly fundamentalist apologists, continue to rely *heavily* on Baconianism to explain things like the age of the earth and the pre-Adamite world, as well as to offer physical proof of the resurrection and other phenomena that are sacred to our faith.

I am grateful for the efforts of our fundamentalist brothers and sisters who have engaged Scripture using Baconianism to push back Darwinism and the evolutionary hypotheses that have assaulted our faith, particularly in the universities. I'd like to suggest that intellectualism, as successful as it has been to defend the faith, is not enough to make for a robust, totally satisfying faith.

Put simply: apologetic channels on YouTube are not the final stop. Saints who binge their favorite apologists should, at some point, sense dissatisfaction, even wonderment, about what's beyond intellectual investigation of the divine.

I speak from experience. Hundreds of Allison-like questions had piled up over a ten-year period. To process them, I started to explore the question of theodicy—the philosophy of explaining how God's goodness and justice can be vindicated despite the existence of evil and suffering.

I assumed I could find answers through a rational, empirical pursuit, like a detective in search of evidence for the truth. All I needed was time. Absorbed in the pursuit during a long, tedious flight, I concluded that the project of theodicy is a cat's game. It is self-defeating. There's no satisfying theodicy.

Suffering is a mystery. A *mystery*!

At some point, those studying theodicy will begin to fabricate ideas to satisfy their ideas. Here is where theodicy becomes dangerous. These fabrications create intellectual dishonesty and even an unethical theology.

---

1. C. Leonard Allen, "Baconianism and the Bible in the Disciples of Christ: James S. Lamer and 'The Organon of Scripture,'" *Church History*, vol. 55:1, March 1986, 66. For more on Baconianism, common sense reasoning, and the Enlightenment, see Kenneth J. Archer, *A Pentecostal Hermeneutic: Spirit, Scripture and Community* (Cleveland, TN: CPT Press, 2009), 48–54.

Theodicy creates more harm than good. I'm unconvinced that it's helpful in the least.[2] Imagine the hack job I'd have done trying to vindicate Allison's mom's untimely death. I doubt any scanty explanation would have empowered Allison to serve Christ more faithfully. If anything, it would disappoint her faith. In cases like these, intellectualism must give way to *mystery*, as painful as it might be for the theorist to concede.

Intellectualism that fails to accept the place *mystery* holds within the faith, counting it an adversary, produces an artificial and even injurious faith. G. K. Chesterton understood this when he wrote:

> Mysticism keeps men sane. As long as you have mystery, you have health; when you destroy mystery, you create morbidity. The ordinary man has always been sane because the ordinary man has always been a mystic. He has permitted the twilight. He has always had one foot in earth and one foot in fairyland…The morbid logician seeks to make everything lucid and succeeds in making everything mysterious. The mystic allows one thing to be mysterious, and everything else becomes lucid.[3]

Those relying too heavily on Western intellectualism would do well to reawaken the element of mystery. Offer mystery an empathetic place in your contemplation of the divine, if for no other reason than because mystery is a crucial element of Christian doctrine and thought.[4]

David Hume, one of Christianity's notorious critics, had no trouble recognizing the place mystery holds within church history and thought. He denounced theology for having an "appetite for absurdity and contradiction" and accused clergy of suppressing reason with "the most unintelligible sophisms." He jested, "Will you set up profane

---

2. See Sari Kivistö and Sami Pihlström, *Kantian Antitheodicy: Philosophical and Literary Varieties* (London, UK: Palgrave Macmillian, 2016), 4. The authors point out that philosophical and moral approaches to theodicy are "insincere" and even "morally scandalous." They suggest that suffering doesn't have to be, and shouldn't be, approached theoretically because rational theodicies fail to acknowledge the suffering individual, their experience, and the sincerity of that experience.
3. G. K. Chesterton, *Orthodoxy* (New Kensington, PA: Whitaker House, 2013), 25–26.
4. See William J. Wainwright, "Theology and Mystery," in Thomas P. Flint, ed., *The Oxford Handbook of Philosophical Theology* (Oxford, UK: Oxford University Press, 2009), 78.

reason against sacred mystery? No punishment is great enough for your impiety."[5]

Hume was right about one thing: mystery *is* central to Christianity. Clergy throughout Christian history actually prove what Hume meant as criticism. Pseudo-Dionysus the Areopagite, a late fifth century theologian, begins his *Mystical Theology* by acknowledging mystery and praying for the Triune God's guidance:

> Triad supernal, both super-God and super-good…direct us aright to the super-unknown and super-brilliant and highest summit of the mystic Oracles, where the simple and absolute and changeless mysteries of theology lie hidden within the super-luminous gloom of the silence, revealing hidden things, which in its deepest darkness shines above the most super-brilliant, and in the altogether impalpable and invisible, fills to overflowing the eyeless minds with glories of surpassing beauty.[6]

Julian of Norwich, a fourteenth-century English anchoress, considers mystery quite often in *Showings*. She sets the knowability of God into tension with the unfathomable:

> For everything which the simple soul understood, God wants that to be revealed and known; for he himself, powerfully and wisely, out of love, hides the things which he wishes to be secret. For I saw in the same revelation that there are many hidden mysteries which can never be known until the time when God in his goodness has made us worthy to see them. And with this I am well satisfied, waiting upon our Lord's will in this great marvel.[7]

Ephrem the Syrian, a fourth-century theologian and saint, implores his hearers to respect mystery upon approaching the Godhead. He warns of the limitations of investigation, such as measuring the fountain from which we drink, as he puts it:

---

5. David Hume, *The Natural History of Religion* (London: A. & H. Bradlaugh Bonner, 1757).
6. *Dionysius the Areopagite part I Divine Names, Mystical Theology, Letters, &c.*, trans. by Rev. John Parker (London: James Parker and Co., 1897), 130.
7. Julian of Norwich, *Showings* trans. by Edmund Colledge and James Walsh (Mahwah, NJ: Paulist Press, 1978), 259.

Let there be stillness
Among the orators;
Let there be silence
Among the investigators,
Respecting hidden mysteries! …

But an occasion hath arisen,
To throw this into confusion;
"For it is proper," they say,
"That we should scrutinize these *Names*,
In order that we may comprehend them."

Captious enquiry hath now begun:
Disputation hath entered:
War is commenced:
And the truth has fled away!

It is therefore preferable,
That without research,
We should possess the Truth;
Than that by such research
We should want it altogether.

Again, it is better
That in simplicity
We should inherit life;
Than that by much knowledge
We should inherit death.

It is also preferable
In the time of thirst,
To drink of the waters;
Than, instead of drinking,
To measure the fountain.

It is far better,
For a young child,
To recognize his father,
By actual vision;
Than by investigation.

It is likewise better,
By constant guidance
Of a *true* faith,
To learn the Truth,
Without curious enquiry.[8]

Pseudo-Dionysus, Julian of Norwich, Ephrem the Syrian, and other theologians throughout church history aren't against intellectual pursuit—as long as one understands that Christianity is a long shot away from being captured into tidy propositions. Eighteenth century revivalist and Yale graduate Jonathan Edwards, for example, acknowledges the limits of his own brilliance and appeals to mystery, particularly in connection to the Trinity. He felt the more one explained it, the more mysterious it became.[9]

I'm not calling for fewer apologists. I am calling for more mystics, though I use the word conservatively and carefully, owing in large part to the objections that Protestant theologians such as Emil Brunner, Reinhold Niebuhr, and even Martin Luther himself have had with the word.[10]

What *I* mean by a *mystic*, regardless of what others have meant, is one who is aware—while doing theology and working out their faith—that Christian doctrine and ritual involve enigmatic realities that can only be known through the work of the Holy Spirit. A mystic experiences God while participating in these mysteries and understands that trying to explain them with certainty is profane.

---

8. "On the Mystery of the Trinity," in *Select Metrical Hymns and Homilies of Ephraem Syrus* trans. by the Rev. Henry Burgess (London: R. B. Blackader, 1853), 135–138.
9. Jonathan Edwards, "Discourse on the Trinity," in *The Works of Jonathan Edwards* (New Haven: Yale University Press, 1957), xxi, 134, 139.
10. F. L. Cross and Elizabeth A. Livingstone, eds., *The Oxford Dictionary of the Christian Church* (Oxford, UK: Oxford University Press, 2005), 1134.

The church historian Earle E. Cairns notes that mysticism makes a comeback[11] as a result of two things: First, cold intellectualism. Cairns points to the Lutheran Pietist movement that emphasized heartfelt Christian living and personal transformation over scholasticism. Second, crisis. Cairnes connects the popularity of fourteenth-century mysticism with the outbreak of the Black Death (1348–49) and the Peasants' Revolt (1381).[12]

If Cairnes is correct, cold intellectualism, widespread disease, and social unrest become the perfect environment for mysticism to cultivate new adherents. It's not a stretch to suggest that the tightening social unrest of our current society, combined with the aftermath of the COVID-19 pandemic, is enough to humble cold, intellectual Christianity.

Instead of feeling awkward and ashamed about saying, "I don't know," maybe the time is ripe to recover mystery as a holy thing that need not be desecrated with intellectual display.

Might admitting, "I don't know" be the most sacred thing we can do at times? Not as a statement of ignorance, as though we have been apathetic to how the Most High *has* revealed Himself, but rather as an avowal that we only *"know in part"* (1 Corinthians 13:9) and are willing to accept the limits of our humanity.

If that is the case, then "I don't know" isn't the white flag of intellectual surrender but the blindingly bright flag of worship and wonder.

TIPS ON RECOVERING MYSTERY

Here are a few things that will help us to recover mystery. You might find these particularly helpful if you've become weary from intellectualism.

1. OBSERVE THE SACRAMENTS SERIOUSLY

The word *sacrament* comes from a Latin translation of the Greek word *mysterion* (mystery). The standard definition of *sacrament* stems from Augustine of Hippo: it is the visible form of invisible grace. The

---

11. Earle E. Cairns, *Christianity Through the Centuries: A History of the Christian Church* (Grand Rapids, MI: Zondervan, 1996), 242.
12. Ibid.

sacraments are the genuine divine presence of Jesus. In observing them, the believer mysteriously experiences the real and present location of God's abiding grace. God is present in the sacraments. You don't have to *feel* Him. You don't have to rationalize Him. What a relief, especially during crises.

For many of us, this is quite unlike the church of our younger years, where feelings were at a premium, where it was common to question the nearness of God when we couldn't feel or understand Him. In observing the sacraments, we discern, in the paradox of Christ's real presence and mystery, essential elements of the faith, particularly when times are baffling and we don't know...and can't know.

2. BE A CONTEMPLATIVE WONDERER IN YOUR PURSUIT OF GOD

In our investigation of the numinous, we can either be contemplative wonderers or sense-knowledge empiricists. There's a difference:

- The contemplative wonderer's end is to love the things that he discovers. The empiricist's end is only discovery, nothing more.
- The contemplative wonderer accepts the weakness of human reasoning; the empiricist relies on the strength of their human reasoning.[13]
- A contemplative wonderer depends on prayer and grace. Empiricists fall prey to the trap of learning about God *apart* from *loving* God and *needing* God.

Aquinas encouraged wonder. In explaining why Christ wondered, he affirms that it was to teach us to wonder. Wonder is a loving gift that God gave us as a means to be *formed* in Him. Aquinas cites Augustine, saying, "Our Lord wondered in order to show us that we, who still need to be so affected, must wonder."[14] Wonder is formative. It may not lead to a satisfying answer, but there will be growth and formation.

---

13. Charles G. Herbermann et al., *The Catholic Encyclopedia Vol. I–XV* (New York, NY: Universal Knowledge Foundation, Inc., 1913).
14. Thomas Aquinas, *Summa Theologica* trans. Fathers of the English Dominican Province (London: Oates & Wasburne Ltd., 1921), 3.15.8.

3. LOSE THE UNDERGRADUATE SYNDROME

I can expect my undergraduates to come to class on the first day with all the answers. You'd be amazed how much they've figured out from listening to podcasts and YouTube channels. There's no give in their conjecture and absolutely zero mercy for the other side. Little savages. They've single-handedly ended the Calvinism/Arminianism debate, fixed the issues between the Catholic/Orthodox church, and know exactly how the book of Revelation is going to play itself out.

Such certainty is a sign of immaturity. Don't get me wrong, I want my students to be bold about defending the truth that is plain and settled. But being fierce about theological stances that are in flux? It's an unhealthy adoration of the intellect. It's doing cheap theology. It's assuming that human thinking can be used to determine, *exactly* and *comprehensively*, what the Triune God is like. It is "the assumption that our cognitive relation to God, our (best) modes of conceptualization of and thinking about God, are such as to make it possible for us to arrive at the exact truth on such issues."[15]

Keep thinking about God to discover that, for as many things as we know about the Triune God, there is far more mystery than anything we can ever *know*. We have *"all things that pertain to life and godliness"* (2 Peter 1:3), which is significant but it's still a blip in space. That's humbling.

4. CONSIDER APPEALING TO MYSTERY AS A VICTORY, NOT A DEFEAT

The pressure you may feel to explain every jot and tittle of theology is not a virtue of spiritual formation. Ease up. You cannot (and will not) explain everything to everyone all the time. If that's what you thought you could do—or worse yet, think you are currently doing—your theology and spirituality are in trouble.

Wonder more. Acknowledge the paradox. Make room for what Pseudo-Dionysus called "the super-luminous gloom of the silence" in your theological wheelhouse.

---

15. William Alston, "Two Cheers for Mystery!" in Andrew Dole and Andrew Chignell, eds., *God and the Ethics of Belief: New Essays in Philosophy of Religion* (New York, NY: Cambridge University Press, 2005), 99–100.

"I don't know" is a testament to God's vastness. It's also an acknowledgment of your finitude. That's worshipful.

"I don't know." Get used to these three words. They shouldn't sound bleak. They offer the certainty that there's a bigger reality in which we are just a small part.

Why did God allow Allison's mom to die?

I don't know. Baconianism cannot measure the well of life from which I drink.

I'm left to wonder. This leaves room for Him to *fill to overflowing my eyeless mind with glories of surpassing beauty.*

LAST WORDS

You've made it to the end of our starter pack.

We leave you by reemphasizing that these twenty essays by no means exhaust the subjects they have addressed.

If there is anything we've hoped to accomplish, it's getting you to think, *I never thought about it like that. I should learn more*, regarding one of these subjects, a few, or even all of them.

If you haven't already done so, take it upon yourself to do a little digging. Read the Scriptures, of course, but also read some of the books we have cited. Expand your interests, your knowing, and your way of knowing. Grow.

If you find you have taken issue with an essay, that's cool too. Use your angst to press the subject further and discover even more about why you have taken issue. Look, if you can use your disagreement to learn, that's a win. We'll take it. If your aim is our aim, we're on the same team. And there is room for teammates to fuss.

You've been a gracious reader. Thanks for putting up with us.

Yours in Christ,
All of your friends at TheosU

ABOUT THE AUTHORS

Joshua Biedel currently serves as an associate pastor at his church in Sacramento, California, in addition to being a Theos Seminary professor. He previously spent ten years in public education, where he was a vice principal at a classical high school, and teacher of history, philosophy, and English. He holds two master's degrees (in history and teaching) and two bachelor's degrees (in theology and history).

Josh loves to talk about the church, politics, theology, books, movies, history, backpacking, and sports, especially boxing, football, and mixed martial arts. He's unusually obsessed with Virgil, Cicero, and the era of antiquity. You may reach Josh at josh@theosu.ca.

Scott Bolin is a cofounder of Theos Seminary and the founder of Celebration Leadership Institute. He is a thought leader and architect of innovative higher learning in a twenty-first century, post-pandemic world. Scott holds undergraduate and graduate degrees in business from Dallas Baptist University and is currently in pursuit of his doctorate. When not working, Scott is likely chasing one of his three kids or enjoying a movie with his wife Caity.

David H. Campbell holds three degrees in theology from the University of Toronto and the University of Durham, where his research supervisor was Professor C. E. B. Cranfield. David also attended Trinity Evangelical Divinity School in Deerfield, Illinois.

He has authored a number of books, including *Mystery Explained: A Simple Guide to Revelation*; *Landmarks: A Comprehensive Look at the Foundations of Faith*; and *Exodus: The Road to Freedom in a Deconstructed World*. He collaborated with Professor G. K. Beale on *Revelation: A Shorter Commentary*.

David and his wife Elaine spent many years church planting in the UK and Canada. They have eight children and eight grandchildren. They are currently based in Stratford, Ontario, and serve churches and seminaries in many movements across a number of countries.

Gia Chacón is the founder and president of For the Martyrs and March for the Martyrs. She is a humanitarian, public speaker, and bold witness for persecuted Christians around the world. She first began her humanitarian efforts in 2017 and has since traveled to Central America, East Africa, and throughout the Middle East in defense and support of the suffering church.

During her time with the Iraqi and Syrian refugees in Jordan, Gia had the opportunity to speak with them about the atrocities they faced and the horrible acts of violence they suffered for refusing to renounce Christ. After Gia heard these stories, God placed it on her heart to bring greater awareness to the growing crisis of Christian persecution and to use her gifts to make a positive impact in the lives of the suffering faithful. These profound experiences led to the founding of For the Martyrs.

In addition to public speaking, pro-life advocacy, and religious freedom advocacy, Gia is a published writer and has been featured in several national news outlets. She impacts the culture through her social media platforms @genuinelygia. Learn more about For the Martyrs by visiting www.forthemartyrs.com.

Dr. **Christina Crenshaw** has twenty years' experience as a professor, researcher, writer, and biblical justice advocate. As a lecturer at Baylor University, she taught faith and writing, vocational leadership, and human trafficking awareness courses. She also held staff leadership positions as the director of Baylor's leadership minor and as the program director for Truett Seminary's Faith and Sports Ministry.

Dr. Crenshaw has extensive work in anti-human trafficking efforts and justice-based work. She has published and presented on human trafficking prevention education in peer-reviewed journals and at academic conferences. Her abolition and advocacy efforts extend beyond academia. Additionally, Dr. Crenshaw has partnered with several anti-trafficking organizations such as The A21 Campaign, UnBound Now, The Heart of Texas Human Trafficking Coalition, Operation Mobilization's Freedom Climb, and The Texas Governor's Human Trafficking Task Force.

Currently, Dr. Crenshaw serves as an Associate for Cultural Engagement and Leadership at Dallas Theology Seminary's Hendricks Center. She is also a Fellow with Southwestern Baptist Theological Seminary's Land Center for Cultural Engagement. Dr. Crenshaw is passionate about the intersection of the church and culture. She hopes her work encourages the church to do good work for God's glory.

Dr. Crenshaw holds a Ph.D. in Education with a cognate in English from Baylor University. Her undergraduate and master's degrees were earned at Texas A&M University. She also completed a Master of Biblical and Theology Studies at Dallas Theological Seminary. She holds a certificate in apologetics from Biola University and a Texas secondary English teaching certificate.

Gabriel Finochio is a writer, teacher, and preacher. In 2019, he cofounded TheosU with his brother Nathan and brother-in-law, Bryan Vos.

A student of the writings of G. K. Chesterton, Gabriel received his bachelor's degree in theology from Portland Bible College and is currently pursuing his master's in theology. He is on the teaching team at Kings' Church in New York, New York.

In addition to ministry and his work at TheosU, Gabriel runs the edgy, meme-based satire Instagram account @wokejesuschrist, which is not for the faint of heart or those who have no sense of humor. He is unmarried and lives in New York City with his cat, Girl.

John Finochio has been the lead pastor of Crossroads Life Church for twenty-three years. He has been married to the love of his life, Jan, for forty-three years. As a songwriter/musician, John has released three albums of original material, made several appearances on Canadian Christian TV programs, and taught worship seminars and trained worship leaders for over three decades.

His ministry of teaching, preaching, and sensitivity to the Holy Spirit in prophecy has opened many international doors of ministry as well. John serves as the vice chairman of Ministers Fellowship International (MFI) in Canada, a network of ministerial relationships that he and Jan have been a part of for almost thirty years. John is also a regular contributing instructor to the online seminary TheosU, which was founded by his sons and son-in-law in 2019.

John and Jan Finochio have three grown children, Nathan, Gabriel, and Tiffany, and three adorable grandchildren. Apart from ministry responsibilities, John enjoys travelling to warm destinations, playing guitar, reading, watching eclectic classic westerns, exercising, gardening, playing bocce, drinking lattes, Italian cuisine, and trying to beat Jan at Boggle. Readers may email John at finoke1@icloud.com.

Nathan Finochio is the cofounder of TheosU and Theos Seminary. With a heart for the local church, he travels extensively to build up and teach using his humor and unique ability to engage the culture.

Nathan studied at Portland Bible College in Portland, Oregon, and is currently working on his master's degree in theology at Southeastern University. After writing several courses as a teaching pastor in New York for nine years, he began to travel and speak in 2019, which made him realize the need for an online Bible college.

Nathan is also the author of the books *Hearing God: Eliminate Myths. Encounter Meaning* and *Killer Church: Why Some Just Survive and Others Thrive in the Presence of God*. He lives in Franklin, Tennessee, with his lovely wife Jasmine.

Nathan may be reached on several social media platforms as well as his website, www.nathanfinochio.ca.

Elijah Lamb is a viral online Bible teacher who communicates God's Word effectively, especially for Gen Z. His focus is on reaching and discipling his generation through multiple platforms online, as well as in person.

After being saved at age fourteen while on a mission trip, Elijah quickly became passionate about preaching the Word and has been doing so since then. He began preaching online at age sixteen and was traveling by age eighteen, still in his senior year of high school.

Above all, Elijah is most passionate about calling his generation back to the Great Commandment: to love God and desire Him above all else. He wants to see his generation not just saved or even biblically informed, but totally in love with Jesus—that is his greatest goal.

Readers can find Elijah on various social media platforms as well as www.elijahlamb.com.

Landon MacDonald is a pastor from the Phoenix desert and leads a church in Gilbert, Arizona, called Mission. Landon creates weekly content on his popular YouTube channel (Youtube.com/LandonMacDonald), from things as simple as lists of theology topics to as grandiose as purchasing a billboard and interviewing thousands of atheists on Reddit. He has created a series of one hundred short, animated videos about the characteristics of God, as well as a full seventy-two video walkthrough of the entire Bible.

A graduate of Moody Bible Institute, Landon's dream and passion is to demystify the Bible and see people read it and get to know its author, God the Father and the Holy Spirit and its hero, Jesus Christ. Landon also enjoys creating theology memes and is an avid record collector. He loves his wife Bri and their kids Ezra, Violet, and Julian, and playing endless Nintendo games with them.

Austin Molt is a youth pastor from Washington State and is the TheosU "youth pastor." His humor, wit, and sarcasm make him an effective communicator for truth, especially online. He is passionate about helping people go deeper in their understanding of the Bible and leading people to encounter the presence of God.

At an early age, he felt the call of God on his life to preach and has traveled to speak around the nation. Austin started in youth ministry when he was just in high school, and he coaches other youth pastors in building youth ministries that reach young people and raise them up to be disciples.

He has been married to the love of his life, Mckenna, since 2017. They have a daughter named Elliette and just welcomed their son Boden in March 2023.

Austin is a Portland Trail Blazer fan and hopes to one day become a grand master in chess. You can find Austin online at linktr.ee/austinmolt.

Layla Nahavandi is an international preacher, writer, and Bible teacher known for preaching the Word of God with revelation and fire. In 1995, God radically saved Layla's family, who came from a Muslim background. This life-changing encounter gave Layla a passion for taking the gospel of Jesus Christ to the ends of the earth.

Layla is currently completing a Ph.D. in theology focused on the early church. This deep study in theological history stirs her spirit to recover the zeal and power of the early church and fuels her desire to bring revival and reformation to the church of today.

Layla is half-Persian and half-Irish, a British-born, Kiwi-raised Aussie. She has been in full-time ministry for over fifteen years, serving in all sorts of pastoral roles in church life and speaking at churches, camps, conferences, universities, and events across the world. Layla is part of the faculty at TheosU and is also a global evangelist based out of Neuma church in Melbourne, Australia.

To connect with Layla, visit www.laylanahavandi.com.

Corey O'Neill received his bachelor's degree in communication and media studies from Rider University. After a stint as a production assistant, he served as video content creator for New Beginnings Church in Monmouth and Ocean County, New Jersey.

A student at Theos Seminary, Corey blogs about faith and education. He and his wife Sara make their home at the Jersey Shore. You may connect with Corey on Instagram @coreymoneill.

Chris Palmer is the dean of TheosU and Theos Seminary, a Greek scholar, a professor of theology, and the author of a number of books, including *Winks From Scripture: Understanding God's Subtle Work Among Us*; *Greek Word Study: 90 Ancient Words That Unlock Scripture*; *Letters from Jesus: Studies from the Seven Churches of Revelation*; and *Strange Scriptures: Deciphering 52 Weird, Bizarre, and Curious Verses from the New Testament*. Chris is currently working on his PhD at the University of Wales, Bangor (UK).

Chris has travelled to more than forty nations and has helped many congregations grow, flourish, and expand. His desire for missions is to train and educate pastors, encourage congregations, support the vision of the local church, and show the love of God to the culture. He has worked successfully with both traditional churches and the underground, persecuted church.

You may find Chris online at www.chrispalmer.me.

Matt VanNorstran is from Corbin, Kentucky, where he has lived for the past thirty years. He serves the local church in children's ministry and teaching, including the writing of curriculum. Matt holds a bachelor's degree in Bible and theology from Lee University, a Master of Theological Studies from Pentecostal Theological Seminary, and a Master of Theology from Princeton Theological Seminary. He is pursuing his Ph.D. in biblical studies from Bangor University, specializing in Pentecostal approaches to Scripture, specifically the Son of Man in Daniel and the Synoptic Gospels.

Matt is an instructor in the Old Testament and Hebrew for TheosU and Theos Seminary, where he teaches interpretive methodologies. His theological passions include seeking a beneficially appropriate eschatology based in the teleology of creation, as well as making space for Christian spirituality to impact and be impacted by academic study.

Matt also enjoys social media influence, where he is involved with several outlets for education, ministry, and memes. You may contact Matt at matt.van@outlook.com or on Instagram: @mattyveeee.

Bryan Vos is the cofounder of TheosU and Theos Seminary and the mastermind behind the platforms, production, and operations. His passion is to provide quality, affordable theological education through creative innovation and a dash of industry disruption.

Bryan grew up in small towns in Ontario, Canada, immersed in local church ministry, music, and production. His entrepreneurial drive stems from his involvement in various family business ventures from the age of four. He loves the Maple Leafs, the sun, beaching, golf, and green tea.

Bryan and his lovely wife Tiffany have three children: Frankie, Georgie, and Theo.

Stephen Wesley is a pastor, missionary, church planter, and former associate dean. He has been involved in ministry for more than thirty years, travelling to numerous nations, strengthening churches, training leaders, teaching in Bible schools, and ministering at conferences.

His passion in ministry is to strengthen congregations, build up the local church, train and educate pastors, and reveal the love of God to the world. Stephen has worked successfully in both first world and developing-world settings.

A member of the teaching faculty at TheosU and a regular guest lecturer at Life Church College Uganda, Stephen presently leads a missionary itinerant ministry, Beyond Borders Ministries, with his wife Angela.

Stephen is the author of three books: *Cornerstone Truths for the Christian Life*, *Growth and Maturity*, and *Equipped for Fruitfulness*. He is presently editing his fourth book.

You may find Stephen online at beyond-borders.ca; www.instagram.com/stephenwwesley; and www.facebook.com/stephenwwesley.

Thomas West is the pastor of Redeemer Queen's Park (London) and a professor of theology at TheosU. He has a Master of Divinity and a Ph.D. in Systematic Theology from Southeastern Baptist Theological Seminary.

Thomas and his family moved to London in June 2019 to pioneer the planting of a new church community. By God's grace, the church is planted and growing.

Thomas was born and reared in Montgomery, Alabama. After four years at Auburn University, he moved to North Carolina for seminary training. In North Carolina, Thomas was the college/equipping pastor and then discipleship pastor at Providence Church. His ministry focus is on discipleship, leadership development, cultural critique, preaching, and teaching.

Thomas and his wife Elizabeth have two children, Perry Elizabeth and Shepherd. Thomas enjoys reading, occasionally exercising, playing golf, spending time with his family, traveling, and working on a few writing projects. You can keep up with Thomas on Instagram @thomasawest, his family @TheWestLondonLife, and Redeemer Queen's Park @RedeemerQP.

Welcome to Our House!
We Have a Special Gift for You

It is our privilege and pleasure to share in your love of Christian books. We are committed to bringing you authors and books that feed, challenge, and enrich your faith.

To show our appreciation, we invite you to sign up to receive a specially selected **Reader Appreciation Gift**, with our compliments. Just go to the Web address at the bottom of this page.

God bless you as you seek a deeper walk with Him!

WE HAVE A GIFT FOR YOU. VISIT:

whpub.me/nonfictionthx

Whitaker House

www.ingramcontent.com/pod-product-compliance
Lightning Source LLC
Chambersburg PA
CBHW070951180426
43194CB00042B/2248